RUNNING LIKE A GIRL

Defeated by gyms and bored with yoga, Alexandra Heminsley decided to run — with high hopes of attaining the arse of an athlete, the waist of a supermodel, and the speed of a gazelle. Her first attempt did not end well. Yet, six years later, she had run five marathons in two continents. This is not just a book about running. It's about ambition (getting out of bed on a rainy Sunday morning counts), relation-ships (including talking to the intimidating staff in the trainer shop), and your body (your boobs *don't* have to wobble when you run). And it's also about realising that you can do more than you ever thought possible . . .

ALEXANDRA HEMINSLEY

RUNNING LIKE A GIRL

Complete and Unabridged

ULVERSCROFT
Leicester

First published in Great Britain in 2013 by
Hutchinson
London

First Large Print Edition
published 2016
by arrangement with
Hutchinson
The Random House Group Limited
London

A catalogue record for this book is available
from the British Library.

ISBN 978–1–4448–2722–4

Published by
F. A. Thorpe (Publishing)
Anstey, Leicestershire

Set by Words & Graphics Ltd.
Anstey, Leicestershire
Printed and bound in Great Britain by
T. J. International Ltd., Padstow, Cornwall

For my father, who taught me to put one
foot in front of the other.
For my brother, who has kept me going
more times than he can imagine.
And for David, who brought me
sunshine.

Prologue

The secret that all runners keep is that they don't do it for their bodies, but for their minds. Slim legs can get boring, but a clear mind never does. The tight glutes, the xylophone abs, the satisfaction of knowing you can have an extra doughnut in front of the telly: these are not the point of running, but the by-product. The real gold at the end of the rainbow is grasping that you can leave the house almost trembling with trepidation about what lies ahead, and that if you can just keep yourself going, a few minutes, a few lamp-posts, a few kilometres at a time, you will be improving not just your running, but how you live your life.

The moments of anger or desolation that runners experience at desperate points of a lengthy run are basic physiological reactions to the situation. But once you have accepted what they are then you have learned to conquer them, and you will begin to believe anything is possible. A good run when you least want to leave the house has a magical ability to unravel a knotty problem that has been vexing you for days, without you really understanding how. Or it can prompt a depth of emotion you never dreamt you were capable of.

At the end of September last year I went to the cinema in London to watch Ryan Gosling in *Drive*. It's great, I recommend it, but remember: I saw him first. It is hard for me to be distracted when I am in the beam of The Gosling, so when my phone went as I entered the cinema I answered only because it was my sister's due date for her first baby and I could see that it was my mother calling. But instead of being told that my sister had been admitted to hospital, I was told that her husband, a healthy, active 35-year-old, was lying on a ward. His heart rate was dangerously elevated and no one knew why. My mother told me to go into the film as there was nothing any of us could do until he had seen a specialist, but asked me to keep my mobile on in case my sister needed me. I entered the cinema in a semi-trance, my blood icy in my veins.

I sat with my phone in my hand, hypnotised by Gosling, yet aware of a constant ticker tape of anxiety scrolling across my mind. What was happening in the hospital a few miles away? I didn't understand. I texted my father throughout the film, checking to see if there were any updates: no news yet. I left the cinema and telephoned St George's Hospital. I knew that the situation was not good when I was put directly through to my sister within seconds. She was in tears and asked me to come immediately.

What followed was one of the most extraordinary forty-eight hours of all of our lives. I met my sister, headed home, made her some toast and tea, helped her in and out of the bath, and put her to bed. There was no sign of their baby, but nor was there any sign of her husband, who remained attached to myriad mysterious hospital wires. The next morning I accompanied my sister to the midwife, and then to the hospital to see her husband. I looked away when he told her that he was going into emergency heart surgery in a matter of hours. I held my breath when I heard him ask the surgeon what the alternative was. I did not breathe out when the reply came. 'There is none. Your condition is very rare, and fatal if untreated.'

My sister was advised to go home and rest while the surgery took place, and that the procedure would take two to three hours. Resting was easier said than done; it took us ten minutes to get her upstairs, wracked as she was with sobs of despair. I went downstairs and made three dishes of lasagne, wishing I had my trainers. I was still wearing the same outfit I'd left for the cinema in the previous day.

Four hours later we had heard nothing. My sister sat at the kitchen table and pressed 'redial' for thirty minutes. Eventually we were told we could go and visit. Amazingly her husband was fine, his condition entirely cured by pioneering keyhole surgery. The next morning my sister went into labour and had a beautiful, healthy baby boy: Louis.

★   ★   ★

A week later I ran the Royal Parks Half Marathon in London. There had been a point when I wondered if I'd be able to make it at all, but in the end it seemed like the only sensible thing to do. The previous week had been spent in a flurry of emails and phone calls, recounting the story of the extraordinary turn of events again and again. I visited the family, I visited my friends, I visited everyone I loved and could reach. I wanted to hug them all. And at every visit I told the story over and over until it was ragged, worn away by retelling, until it started to seem like a plotline from a soap opera I was summarising for a fellow viewer on Twitter. It was almost as if it hadn't happened to me.

I was nervous the morning of the run, as I

always am when I go to a big public event alone. Had I forgotten something? Who would get me home to Brighton if I fell? Would this finally be the race where I wet myself in front of a crowd of onlookers? The usual worries. But, race aside, I felt happy and relaxed after a week in the company of those I loved, digesting the dramatic but ultimately joyous news.

As I crossed the starting line I felt a little emotional at how beautiful London looked that day. It had been a bizarre year for weather, and while there had been rain that morning, there was now a gorgeously crisp autumn sky and the leaves in Hyde Park were exquisite. I felt a little lump in my throat as we left the park and headed out along the Mall, then down along the river. We crossed at Waterloo Bridge and began to run back. That was when it happened. The tears.

Initially I thought it was just a tiny eye leak, the kind you might get at a moving political speech, a great novel or the last half-hour of *Children in Need*. You know, if you've had the right amount of whisky and some good company. A moment in passing. But I was wrong. The tears that could initially be disguised as eyes-streaming-from-the-cold soon turned into heaving sobs.

The first one appeared as a sort of

half-gulp, half-yelp. The second one was an identifiable gasp. Then, five miles into a half marathon, I was off — proper full-blown crying. At first I didn't know what was wrong with me: I simply wasn't sad, in fact I was very happy. The news was all good, wasn't it? Yet it seemed that after almost a fortnight of coping, my body and mind suddenly decided to unburden at mile five, in the anonymity of the crowd. Only I wasn't anonymous; I was wearing a top bearing my nickname, HEMMO, in eight-inch letters. But by the time I had realised this, a thousand feelings per second had started to course through me, as if I were some sort of magical emotion-kaleidoscope. Every other second came a fresh sensation I hadn't let myself feel in front of my sister, the surgeons or anyone in the hospital. It was a tidal wave of tears.

Before I knew it my sobs were almost uncontrollable, to the point where the steady rhythm of my feet on the pavement had become the only thing stopping me from losing it altogether. I don't know how I managed to keep running, yet it was all that I could do. The memories of the previous ten days flashed before me: my hand round my mobile in that dark cinema as I waited for news, my sister's hand as she signed the consent form for her husband's surgery, my brother-in-law's hand as he stroked her bump. The smell of the antiseptic in the hospital, the smell of the food I made while my sister slept, the smell of my newborn nephew's head. Flashes of those conversations I had been having for days on end, until they lost all meaning to me, flooded back into my consciousness: 'What, he could have died?' 'What, the baby was born the next day?' 'What, you're still going to run at the weekend?'

Of course I still ran, because it was only through running that I was able to process how traumatic those few days had been. Except, of course, the spectators along the route that day didn't know the reason for my sobs. They just saw a runner in distress and cheered me on. Which, if I am honest, only made things worse. Because with every step my heart seemed to be swelling — expanding to make room for this newly realised love I felt for my brother-in-law, my new nephew and the friends that had supported us all. There simply wasn't space to love the sweet faces of the children who had come out to support a dad or a sibling and found themselves cheering me along too. Was there? So their kindness was converted into more grinning tears, as I gulped and tried to smile back and explain: 'Oh no, don't worry, I'm fine! It's just that . . . ' and I was past them.

'WELL DONE, HEMMO,' they shrieked at my back. And that just made me cry more.

Calm down, you're embarrassing yourself now, you need to get your heart rate down if you're going to carry on, I told myself, which only prompted further tears at the very thought of hearts. *Oh hearts! Hearts are so amazing!* Once again I was lost in emotion at the wonder of life itself.

I don't remember the last couple of miles, until I reached the final straight. I saw the finish line and suddenly felt a strength I didn't know I had. Admittedly I had not run exceptionally fast, given my busy schedule of weeping, but suddenly I felt more powerful than ever before. My brother-in-law had survived. My sister had survived. We had all survived. So I sprinted. I felt myself speed up, until I could see that I was overtaking the people around me. I left them behind, running faster than I ever had. Slowly I felt my face begin to tingle, then my hands. As I came within metres of the finish line I wondered if I was going to make it at all. But I did, straight into the arms of a St John's Ambulance worker who had seen me coming. He tilted my head forward over my knees to steady my breathing, which was now hysterical. I thanked him through my weird gulpy gasps, and with relief took the water he gave me. Moments later my brother appeared and bought me a sausage in a bun. It was the best sausage in a bun I have ever known, and they are *always* good. On the train home I emailed my girlfriends the story of what had happened, expecting to be told I was quite mad. But they understood. They understood it all.

That day in October was the day that taught me most about why I run: once you've experienced the delicious realisation that you can carry on when you are quite sure you are about to die of tears in a crowd of thousands, you have taught yourself a skill that is applicable to all of life. It turns out that to survive, you just have to keep going.

PART 1

'It's the most natural thing in the world. We were born to run.'

'You just put on your trainers and head out the door, that's the beauty of it.'

'It's just you, the road and your thoughts.'

These are the things that people say about running. These are lies.

Running is awful. It feels unnatural, unnecessary, painful. It can hijack you with breathlessness, cripple you with panic and overwhelm you with self-consciousness. It isn't a warm fire or a deep sofa or a cup of tea and a smile. It is cold and hard and unforgiving. It feels more difficult the better you get. It hurts your head and it hurts your toes.

But it is also the pleasure of being outside on a sunny day, feeling the prickle of the sun on your skin. It is the delight of feeling your body temperature rise despite the crisp winter breeze against your face. It is feeling blood rush around every part of your body and coming home to a welcoming bath and a delicious curry, your skin still glowing an hour later.

And, as I have learned, it is also an honour, a privilege and a gift.

So this part of the book isn't about trying to persuade you that you should run, but that you can. I was there, repulsed and intimidated by the beatific smiles and radiant smugness of the determinedly Sporty Types. For years running seemed a punishment to keep off the pounds — yet another way we were being told to keep off the pounds, to feel the burn, to pay for that half glass of white wine and four squares of chocolate. God forbid we might have a body that was less than beach ready!

I could remember how everything just felt more fun when I ran as a child but there didn't seem to be much to encourage me, a woman in her thirties, who'd spent several years forgetting supper on a Friday in place of a night out, that it could be something for me. So, this book is the one I didn't have but would have liked to have read before I went on my first (disastrous) run. Something for those people who think they can't run for whatever reason. For the women who think they aren't slim enough to wear running kit or that it's not worth it if they don't want to complete an entire marathon, for the women who think that running around in circles is an idiotic way to spend the best part of an hour.

For those women who don't yet trust that it really is a source of immeasurable pleasure, self-belief and unexpected companionship, rather than a necessary purgatory — that they might, just might, enjoy the confidence, the physical ease or the mental clarity that running brings.

Because it was in running that I discovered that the scope of our achievements is not determined by others, but by ourselves.

1

Not Born to Run

'Only those who dare to fail greatly can ever achieve greatly'
                    Robert F. Kennedy

That was it, I was going to run round the block. I had high hopes: hopes of the arse of an athlete, the waist of a supermodel and the speed of a gazelle. Defeated by gyms, bored by sanctimonious yoga teachers and intimidated by glossy tennis clubs, I decided it was time to end a lifetime spent believing myself to exist on the outside of sport. I would return powerful and proud, the city still reeling at the sight of my grace and speed on the pavements of Kilburn. This is the story of my first run.

There was little else I could do to procrastinate. The washing-up was done, the ironing was pancake flat, the bookshelves dusted. Every possible worst-case scenario had been replayed in my head a million times, and it was clearly never going to rain. I had run out of excuses. I tied back my hair,

17

grabbed a 500ml bottle of water, put my keys in the pocket of my tracksuit bottoms, and stood at the front door. This was it. I was going for a run.

I opened the front door and walked down the three steps to the pavement. What was I supposed to do next? Perhaps some stretching? I held on to a lamp-post and pulled my foot up behind me, trying to stretch the front of my thigh. I did the same thing with the other leg and looked around anxiously. My heart was beating too fast already. What if someone could tell it was my first run? Would they be able to see that I was doing it wrong?

Running. It was just running, I told myself. I set off down the road, trying to look to the Saturday passers-by as if this were something as normal to me as taking the bins out. But that road was a long road. It was the grouting between the urban delights of Kilburn High Road and the chic coffee shops of Queen's Park. As I headed towards the park, the houses became progressively more glamorous and well groomed. I, however, did not.

I was halfway down the road when I had to stop. There was an awful juddering as the whole world moved up and down on account of my lumbering limbs: thud, thud, thud as my feet hit the ground, sending shockwaves through both my body and the pavement.

Within seconds — not even minutes — my face had turned puce with intense heat and my chest was heaving. I could see the crossroads, but to my ragged humiliation I could not make it that far. I was not just out of breath, I was actually having to swallow down panic to keep myself moving at all.

I walked for the length of the next song on my playlist. The indignity of admitting I could no longer run seemed slightly less than that of the physical wreck I would become if I continued to run. Eventually I made it to the park and tried to run for the length of the next song. I could not manage even that and I ended up walking past the field of children playing football at the centre of the park. Each of them seemed to be darting around effortlessly, continually in motion, while every part of my body seemed to be seizing up.

The wobble of my thighs, the quake of my arse, the ridiculous jiggle of my boobs, they seemed to mock me as the Saturday dads stared in horror from the playground. Every time my feet struck the tarmac I was convinced my ankle would twist, and every time I looked down to check I was confronted with the expanse of my thigh looming towards me. It felt as if my physical self was entirely disconnected from everything my intellectual or emotional self was trying to tell it. *Calm down, putting in the effort is the main thing,* was merely met with, *Yeah right, because putting yourself in this much pain is a great idea.* Which in turn stole away any possibility of calming down with the result that my heart rate started rising from fear once again.

As I reached the far end of the park and turned to head back, the pounding of my heart and then the slow fire in my lungs convinced me of that one immovable fact: I would never make it home.

Eventually, after several more starts and stops and a total avoidance of eye contact with every single person I passed, I got home. I rewarded myself handsomely with a phenomenal amount of food and drink at the party that night, blithely telling everyone that I'd been for a huge run that morning. When I woke up the next morning I felt as if I had been run over by a truck. A big truck with huge, grooved tyres. Oh, this was an unacceptable way to make oneself feel, I declared. I must have overtrained. Later I looked up how far I had run: it was one mile.

It was another three months before I tried to run again.

★ ★ ★

I don't remember making the decision that I couldn't run; it was simply one of those things that made me *me*, like my love of cheese, or my distaste for men in polo necks.

But my certainty that I couldn't run was absolute, my envy profound of those who could and my admiration for my flatmate boundless. She would appear at the front door, glowing from one of her regular routes around Regent's Park or Hampstead Heath, and I would welcome her enthusiastically. We'd chat about what she'd seen, her leaning at the kitchen counter sipping a glass of water, me on the sofa with my laptop propped on my knees like a windy baby.

'I wish I could run.' There is a certain comfort in saying it aloud. 'It looks like so much fun,' I'd sigh as she took off her trainers. I felt a twinge of sadness knowing that it was too late for me to start. I would reach for the TV remote with resignation.

As I watched my flatmate's running kit circulating hypnotically in the washing machine, I never questioned the casual lunacy of my conviction that I 'couldn't run'. It seems to have been cumulative, something that I let happen to me, a state of affairs I succumbed to without question.

I remember being six or seven, and running being what I could barely wait to do during break time at school. And I remember being thirty, having total confidence that running was utterly beyond me.

Somehow, during the years in between, I forgot the sensation of reading or being read to in infant class, and beginning to feel that familiar itch in my legs. I would look up at the clock, back at the teacher and out of the window. Soon. Then, the very second the bell went, we would grab our coats and head outside to play whatever game we could think of, just as long as it meant running around for a bit. We didn't call it running at that age, because running was how we did everything, mittens trailing from our sleeves and plaits whipping at our cheeks. We were just children doing our thing, and our thing was always more fun when done at speed. We ran and we laughed. They were one and the same.

As a ten-year-old I stood daydreaming at the start of the 400-metres circuit. I watched the warm summer sun shine through the pinprick holes in my navy blue Aertex shirt, noticing how it had browned both my arms and the grass of the track. I would merrily run round it for as long as I could, sometimes straight across the middle if I fancied a change, until we were called back to lessons or until someone else needed the track.

Twenty years later I was completely at ease

with my status as someone who lived on the outside of sport. It was as if I had never run. It never occurred to me that I could, that all I had to do was to leave the house. I wasn't a runner and that was that. Somehow I had lost sight of the fact that not being a runner and not being able to run were not one and the same.

I wasn't the sporty type, it was as simple as that. I was a curvy girl with little or no competitive spirit. I rarely made connection between bat and ball during games at school, and neglected my body almost entirely for three years at university. Perhaps I broke into a run that time I was pushing my friend Clare down Cotham Hill in a shopping trolley, and I know I danced on a podium a few times, but they were definitely the sum of my collegiate athletic endeavours.

Then I moved to London and joined the eternal treadmill of private gym membership. Each time I looked round a new venue I told myself that this would be the one. This would be the gym that would make me fall in love with exercise. But they never did. Once the oleaginous buzz of viewing the facilities, being given my workout profile and trying the steam room for the first time was over, the magic quickly faded and I returned to fleeting, guilty glimpses at my bank statement as I realised each visit was costing me more and more.

Back then I didn't know that the gym was just sticky methadone to the heroin of running outdoors. How could pounding along on the running machine, going nowhere in front of a wall of relentless rolling news, compare to the freedom of running along the seafront, looking up at a seagull hovering over a scrap of food on the path and realising that for a moment you were neck and neck? But still I continued. Next came the (Madonna-influenced) yoga phase. Hours of bending and sweating in a room full of freelance web designers and stressed-out fashion editors. Then came pilates, and even a flirtation with meditation.

Finally, after a summer of heartache, followed by almost crippling depression, came the walking phase. After a hectic routine of lying under my coffee table weeping, I had reached a point where I just had to get outside and see daylight. I wanted to feel the breath of warm air on my skin, I yearned to feel my blood actually circulate round my body again, and I needed to do it with a view that was not just that of a prefab ceiling tile or a yogi's tatty three-week-old pedicure. Half-deranged by weeks of erratic sleeping — nights spent enervated and

24

panicky followed by sluggish, heavy-limbed days — I decided in desperation that physically exhausting myself might make the nights seem a little more welcoming. I longed to long for my bed, instead of seeing it as a battleground for a never-ending war against my own demons. I yearned to yearn to go and lie down at the end of the day, legs aching from use rather than the frantic jiggling they did under my desk for hours on end.

One day I just upped and left the house, and didn't return until nearly dusk. Thus began my walking phase. I would walk for hours, all over the routes that my now ex-flatmate had covered the year before. Hampstead Heath, Regent's Park, Hyde Park. I would leave the house on a Sunday morning and not return for three or four hours. Often I could barely remember the time I had spent away, as if the meditative repetition of my strides had somehow hypnotised me. I would begin firey, anxious to get away from the dirty urban streets, the dawdling pedestrians, the local shops whose owners had seen me tear-stained and bedraggled over my summer of bad eating. Then, as the parks opened up before me, I would feel my spirits lift. I would romp around the Heath, deliberately choosing to get lost a while in a wooded area I didn't recognise. I would stroll through rose

25

gardens wondering if I would ever know the stories behind the blooms' names. A tiny part of the me I thought I had lost started to wriggle back to the surface.

I would arrive home exhausted but noticeably lighter of spirit. My head felt as if someone had popped in and run a duster around it. I formed a truce with my bed, seeing it as a place for rest anew. I cherished the time I spent off grid, uncontactable and alone. The coils that had spent endless nights tightening in my mind would loosen a little; my imagination felt itself inclined to wander towards the positive rather than the self-focused disaster movie scenarios it had recently felt so devoted to. I remain convinced that those walks in the summer of 2006 saved me. Not just because they restored my ability to sleep, but because they delivered me that first tiny germ of physical confidence. If I could walk for four hours what might happen if I sped up . . . and then sped up even more? My heart had begun to believe that anything was possible, and my head had begun to plan for it. Maybe even . . . a run.

So it was this spirit of optimism that inspired that first run to Queen's Park a year later. If my heart could survive the pummelling it had taken, my legs must surely have more to give. I figured that if I'd been taking three-hour walks regularly for about a year, I *might* be ready for a run. My preparations were extensive: first there were two weeks of thinking about it. What would it feel like? Would I fall over? How would I get home if it were too much? I was filled with positivity and enthusiasm. Hours were spent checking out potential new fitness clothes for the 'new me'. I panicked, then became exhilarated, then put it off for a couple more days. Thus continued the loop for a whole fortnight in the run-up to that unholy day.

When the morning of The Run came I woke up and immediately ate three slices of toast with honey, 'for energy'. Then I spent at least ninety minutes faffing around on iTunes, trying to compose a playlist of such magnitude that it would propel me round the park, no matter how debilitating I found the experience. Despite my research I had not dared to buy anything new to wear. Instead I dug out some old tracksuit bottoms, last worn when I'd had adult mumps and watched two *Sopranos* boxsets on a single weekend. I rifled through my drawers until I found a bra that covered as much of me as possible, somehow hoping to avoid a level of jiggle that marked me out as too much of an amateur. And I found some old trainers in the back of my cupboard beneath some festive reindeer antlers.

And then I hit the streets — and failed. It was a Saturday in August, the month of my sister's wedding. It was sunny but not too hot, perfect running weather. That afternoon I was heading to Norfolk with my family for a party for wedding guests who wouldn't be able to make it to the ceremony, which was to be held abroad. It was the perfect time to get in shape, I told myself. After all, the big day was coming up in a couple of weeks and I had bribed myself to take that first run on the grounds that it would mean I could really get involved with the party food later; that amidst the happy chaos of the family wedding to come, I'd have the promise of an empowering new hobby to return to. My disappointment could not have been sharper.

When I returned home that Saturday I was nearly broken in both body and spirit. While my lungs and legs were wracked with pain, my mind was working even harder at inflicting a thousand tiny blows. Was this what running was really going to feel like now? Would every run mean confronting this heinous combination of shame, pain and rage? Why did people do this? Why did I want to do it? What part of myself was I hoping to access? Was it slimness or achievement?

Chastisements rained down upon doubts as I sat, wretched in the bath. After that disastrous first attempt these thoughts wedged themselves at the back of my mind for months, like a pen behind an old radiator. Always out of reach I could never quite deal with them, but nor were they ever quite silent.

My sister's wedding came and went in what felt like an ecstatic flash. My reaction to the multiple photographs of me, however, was less joyful. Instead of the confident curves I'd always seen myself as having, I realised that part of the juddering agony of that first run was down to the fact that I had undeniably put on weight. Running would help with this weight, but this weight did not help with running.

I began to understand what other women meant when they talked about feeling trapped in their own bodies. Those magazines I would sniff at in railway stations and doctors' waiting rooms were full of them. But I used to think I would never become one. Until I found myself watching runners with increasing longing, wondering what their secret was, how they knew what to do, what got them going. And yet running still seemed an impossibility. Everyone has limitations and I had reached mine. There was no way I could deal with endless repeats of that Saturday morning experience, so it was best to try and forget about it altogether.

I did my best, until my siblings and I went to go and stay with my parents one weekend. My brother casually mentioned that he was going to apply for a place in the London Marathon.

'Wow!' I gasped. 'How amazing to be able to do that! I was so surprised when I went to cheer on a friend, it's such an emotional event.'

'You should do it too then,' said my father. His voice didn't flicker. His eyes didn't look up from the cup of coffee he was making. His hands remained steady at the task. All very well coming from a man who'd run several marathons when we were children, but this was me we were talking about.

'Don't be ridiculous!' I exclaimed. 'I can't run.'

'You don't run,' corrected my father. 'But you're more than able.' There was no doubt in his voice, not even a shadow of it. Suddenly, hearing it from someone else made me realise: there was nothing stopping me from running but me.

And that was that. The seed was planted.

The next morning I announced that I was not to be broken. Indeed, I would Run Again. At this point I started making a kerfuffle on a scale that suggested I was actually planning to run home from South Wiltshire to North London. I commandeered my father's computer for hours, Googling 'small run Northwest London', 'how to know if you can do 5 km', 'supplies needed for 5km run' and various permutations of the same. I downloaded maps, I discussed nutrition and running style with my brother and I chatted about trainers and bras with my sister. Eventually, somewhat exasperated, my father explained that I had two working legs, no medical problems and a lot of long walks under my belt. He reminded me that it would only be about half an hour anyway, before adding, 'If you get tired, you just walk. You know you can do that.'

It was afternoon before I returned to London. By the time I got to Regent's Park Tube station night had fallen, but instead of being scared I hugged the darkness to me, relieved that no one would be able to see the fear on my face. I crossed into the park, made sure no one was around and set off.

At first it was exactly like the last time: the burning, the panting, the panic. But this time there were two key differences: I was not in my neighbourhood so there was little chance of running into anyone I knew, and I was running a loop so I *had* to get back to where I had started from. Then, after about twelve minutes, a miracle: it got easier. My heart rate, while still high, started to even out. Instead of feeling like a never-ending heaven-bound roller-coaster that would only ever go up, it became steady. The two beats of my feet started to match the two beats of my breathing — in and then out. I was doing it. Yes, my legs were hurting. Yes, I was still scared that I would never make it all of the way round the park. But yes! I was running.

By the time I got home from my second run I was awash with a heady cocktail of endorphins and undiluted smugness. I did some ostentatious stretching with my lights on and curtains open, took a bath (curtains closed) and ate a bowl of pasta approximately the same size as my sister's wedding cake.

It was as if I were experiencing a reverse hangover. The wondrous, magical, heady phase of being drunk lasts for such little time — an hour, perhaps three at best, before it melts into discomfort, delirium or just plain boredom. Yet the hangover can last a day or two. Finally I could see with startling clarity that the time I had spent experiencing any pain on account of running was embarrassingly outweighed by the amount of time that I felt good about it. I was aglow. I was invincible. I was thinking I might be able to do it again.

One of the only concrete pieces of advice my father had given me the weekend before was to keep a running diary, so that I could remind myself how I felt after different runs. When I look at that first entry it says this:

18th October 2007
5k round Regent's Park
5.45–6.20 p.m.
So exhausted after 12 mins but then it seemed okay. Had breath back by RP tube, so ran home from QP as well. Felt so much easier than expected. Might go again!

The next day I applied for the London Marathon.

2

Learning to Run

'Anybody can be a runner. We were meant to move. We were meant to run. It's the easiest sport.'

Bill Rodgers

I did not know these things then, on those early runs, but the subsequent acceptance of my marathon application meant that there was no turning back. I was committed to running regularly, despite having little or no idea what I was doing. Pushing the practicalities aside I focused on the marathon as a goal and used that as a motivator. I had been to cheer friends on in the past and been moved by the sight of so many humans trying their very best at something. As with the practicalities I ignored the memories of men running by with chafed-to-bleeding nipples and feeling quite faint from the heat of a particularly hot April's day despite being a spectator, standing entirely still. I would cross the finish line proud, I was sure of it.

To my consternation it seemed that others

were not so sure. It appeared that the idea of me running was not worth the interest to some, yet hilarious to others, whose reaction to news of my new hobby was either: 'You're doing what?', or: 'Yeah, good luck with that!' and the odd 'Ha ha ha, we'll believe it when we see it.' Then there was the email from my friend Vanessa, who worked for Sense, the charity I was now running for, delicately reminding me that what I had just committed to doing for her was 'quite hardcore'. Most were encouraging, including my family, but their responses did little to quell the increasing suspicion that I had taken on something insane, something undoable, something that remained indisputably 'not me'.

Each time I told someone about the project I found myself needing a little extra steeliness, as the reactions came back an almost undiluted mixture of mirth and disbelief. Why the hilarity? I found myself wondering time and again. It's just running, surely there's a cap on how funny that can be?

The peculiar combination of determination and terror that all this created did not prove easy to forget. Every time I gritted my teeth, determined to do things properly despite the sniggers, I was seized by fear and acute self-awareness. As a child I was unselfconscious, my arms and legs were just extensions of toys that I could employ for my own amusement. My childhood memories of sport were of standing in sunny fields playing rounders, waiting patiently for a ball to come my way, or leaping around a netball court filled with boundless energy.

It was the post-adolescent sports years that haunted me. When, at twelve or thirteen, my body suddenly started to change I felt utterly alien from it, as if I'd been deposited in another being's skin entirely. I grew so fast that I spent the best part of a summer in the 1980s crying with pain. It was a wretched holiday that I spent sitting on a sandy beach, watching my brother and sister play, as the ratcheting pain of my knees stretching to accommodate my now larger limbs preoccupied every inch of my mind and body.

It was at this age that my clumsiness began. At first my family were sympathetic when I would get up to leave a room and hit a table or a door handle with my hip. Until it started to happen several times a day. Just passing the salt across the dinner table involved knocking over a full water glass with my new boobs, or swiping at a jar of ketchup with my suddenly longer arms. I felt like a renegade forklift truck driver on their first day at work, numbly trying to control a series of mechanisms I was far from adequately trained to operate.

Sport became torture. After years of coping with rounders and netball at prep school, my new school served indigestible servings of lacrosse and tennis. The other girls in my class seemed to grow stronger and slimmer as I became more curvy and unwieldy. My body, once a source of such fun, was now more of an unreliable straitjacket. When I wasn't fretting about how it looked I was worrying about what shape it might be next. But I still had an enviable weapon in my arsenal: humour. Too proud to let anyone know I cared and too young to worry about lack of fitness, I goofed around during sports. I became the class clown on the sports pitch. Take a funny pratfall and no one will mind if you lose the team a goal, I realised. Or mess around enough during tennis lessons then the girls who can really play won't pick you any more.

These were easy lessons to learn and soon I turned those years of loathing into fun again. Here began my tacit acceptance that sport was now 'not for me'. I was one of the funny girls, the clever girls. I didn't have time for those earnest sorts and their sweaty enthusiasm; I'd simply wave cheerily at them from behind a copy of *Just Seventeen* and hope no one would notice that secretly I had lost a little something I used to love. It had slipped, sand-like, from between my fingers before I'd even noticed it was gone.

Now in my thirties I realised I was paying the price for twenty years of playing the clown. For every pratfall I had taken in order to prevent anyone taking me seriously on a sports field, there was now a giggling email. I might have decided I wanted to be taken seriously, but no one else really seemed to be on board with that plan. Despite these reactions there remained a dusty, barely used corner of my mind where I knew I wanted to prove to everyone what I could do. I wanted to be treated like a grown-up, to be believed when I said I had set myself a goal. I wanted to be respected, not just liked. With a marathon I saw my window of opportunity. It was just going to take a *lot* of running.

It was this tiny, gritty speck of determination that kept me going in those early days. In the autumn of 2007 my running diary is filled with entries that say little more than, 'Well, it started fine but then I got INCREDIBLY TIRED,' or, 'My legs felt like actual lead until the last ten minutes — why bother?' or even the charmingly pragmatic, 'This run was so awful I don't want to record it.'

Perhaps I kept this diary because I wouldn't believe I had done the runs unless I did record them. My father had recommended it to me as a way of reminding myself what I thought I was capable of, and seeing it change.

This was a time before smartphones or running apps, so I would map my runs online before leaving the house having scribbled up my arm the order of the street names I needed to follow. But I cared less about getting lost than I did about being seen. There were too many jokes. Phoebe from *Friends*, *Forrest Gump* and *The Littlest Hobo*. They all haunted me as I scuttled through side streets, residential roads and the shadiest corners of local parks, convinced that all passers-by could spot my rookie status from five hundred metres away. Avoiding eye contact with anyone at a pedestrian crossing I kept my cap on and my eyes down, lest I should see one of *those women* summing me up.

It wasn't that I wanted to *be* one of them: the lean, toned women who resembled those in the sportswear catalogues, their golden limbs glinting and their ponytails swishing — it was just that I didn't want to exercise anywhere near them. I would lose concentration on spotting one running towards me, I would feel the tips of my trainers clip the edge of the pavement if one hoved into view as I left a park, I would feel my stride become panicked and irregular if I heard one approaching behind me. After a while though I began to realise that *no one was really watching*. Everyone is ultimately more interested in themselves, their children or their mobile phones. And as I discovered when I started trying to smile at approaching runners, quite a few of them are so tired that they aren't focusing on anything at all.

It amazes me now that I kept leaving the house for those crucial early expeditions, particularly as any potential rewards seemed so far away. I tried whatever I could to maintain momentum for those first few weeks, even though I had no real idea what I was doing. I was still too proud to ask for any advice lest I should give away the extent of how much I cared. Google became my friend, and I would find myself talking online to novice runners on the other side of the country about where specifically their ankles were hurting. I walked and ran, I ran in tiny bursts, I ran after dark when the pavements were emptier. I downloaded podcast after podcast so that I could pretend I was doing 'research for work' while I stomped along in my own sweaty world. I kept going, I kept going, I kept going. Within a month I realised that the first of the rewards was closer than I had ever thought.

I started to lose a bit of weight. That in

turn started to make the running easier. After two or three weeks of doggedly jogging around North-west London I stood on my dusty bathroom scales. 'Oh, I never weigh myself! You can't quantify what I am in kilograms or ounces!' I remembered telling my mother and sister with a flourish the previous Christmas. I looked down at my feet and saw that I had shed a few pounds. Later that week, during an idle moment queueing for the till in my local supermarket, I picked up a kilo bag of potatoes from my trolley. I let its heft sag between my hands, bouncing them slightly, staring at the veg. I had already lost the equivalent of one of those. I imagined the bag strapped round my hips, I imagined me trying to run like that. No wonder half an hour of running already felt easier; there was simply less 'me' to carry around. Slowly the cycle was reversing and the entire task seemed easier. Running began to slide, slowly but surely, along the scale from torment to joy.

What I didn't know on those very first early runs — the ones where even my face seemed to hurt when I got home — was that I wasn't lily-livered or weak-willed. Nor was I biomechanically unable to run. I was in fact 'going lactic'. I had no idea that for a regular pace it takes about ten minutes for the body to start taking on oxygen as fast as it needs it, for one's breathing to regulate or for one's body to be properly warmed up. In fact I had no idea what pace I should be going at all. My goal was simply not to die before the end. For weeks I suspected I was only able to run for ten minutes. I would leave the house and belt out the distance as fast as I thought I could, determined not to walk. Then, exhausted, collapse and descend into existential torment.

I now understand that I was flooding my body with a huge amount of lactic acid, caused by an excess of oxygen in the system. Oxygen is constantly being flushed through our bodies, but if we take it in faster than we can remove it, the surplus sits in our muscles, creating that charming 'run over by a truck' vibe. It stings, it's what makes you hurt from your fingernails to the roots of your hair and beyond. And, crucially, it's what makes so many people give up after three runs. I want to weep when I think of the number of women who head round the block, only to return twelve minutes later, broken and tearful. I don't doubt that when these women meet me and hear that I have run four marathons they want to weep for me as well. I suspect that they believe all runs, for ever, are as crippling as those first few. It's certainly what I thought. They are not. If only someone had told me sooner.

In time, and with some gentle prodding from my father, I came to realise that as 26.2 miles was my goal, I should be trying to steadily increase the distance that I could run, rather than attempting a series of bizarre imaginary sprints around my neighbourhood. So I started to plan each run, first making sure it was a circuit so I was committed to completing it no matter whether I had to stop and walk for sections and secondly increasing the distance incrementally. The thought of getting lost no longer meant getting lost, but the possibility of having to run slightly further than was absolutely necessary. I would recite street names the whole way round, remembering which turn corresponded with which mile, so I could attempt to work out my pace. These days the apps you can download to your phone or iPod are excellent. They calmly talk you through the process of interchanging between walking and running, making sure that your heart rate is raised but has a chance to recover, rather than just blasting on all cylinders and then running out of steam. Six years ago I was trying to figure this out on my own, like a crazed Victorian inventor discovering electricity. But with trainers on.

Despite my ramshackle training plans

largely seeming to work, I was still consumed by ridiculous fears almost every time I reached the end of my road. It was no longer the fear of ridicule, but the idea of running further than I ever had in my life. I'd stand there at the front door, carefully curling my headphone wire round the back of my neck, internally muttering that this would be the one to finish me off: seven miles was definitely the killer, or I must be crazy to contemplate nine and a half.

These ever-more-elaborate disaster scenarios would play themselves out as I approached the limit of what I had run the week before. There were of course the bog-standard trips, sprains and breaks. (Mine were always embellished with some sort of humiliating clothing rip, exposing me to the residents of a particularly chichi street leading off a non-specific Regency park.) There were the Lost Runs, when I would somehow circumnavigate London with no sense of space or time, apparently unable to recognise my surroundings or get home. Then there were the vomiting and diarrhoea terrors. What would happen if I was sick in the street? Or if I needed the loo? Can you actually run while needing a wee without wetting yourself? And what if you eat something untoward and have to pay the lavatorial consequences five miles from home? Would anyone understand? Perhaps greatest of all was my inexplicable yet all consuming fear of dehydration, or hitting The Wall.

It is entirely impossible to read anything about running which does not hammer home the importance of hydration, and there is no literature on marathons that fails to discuss the so-called 'wall', which is the notorious point when your body has expended all of its stored energy and has yet to convert any of the food or drink you've taken. The complete loss of control that these things signified to me were haunting. Scenes would flicker across my mind of my body shutting down as I blacked out from dehydration and exhaustion. My face would go a terrifying putty-grey, my legs would buckle beneath me and I would lie — probably on one of London's most historic streets — foaming at the mouth, flailing, alone. People would laugh and point, sneering, 'That's what happens if you don't train properly,' or, 'She probably didn't have enough water,' and most shaming of all: 'She clearly took on more than she could manage with *that* distance.' There was no doubt in my mind that this would one day happen.

This has never happened.

Things that *have* happened to me are

tripping on a pavement and falling over. I have ripped my running tights; I have realised halfway through a run that the elastic on my running tights has gone; I have got lost, and had to retrace my steps a little; I have become very hot; I have become very thirsty; I have become very tired.

To date neither my bowels nor my bladder have inflicted a roadside betrayal. As a child I often used to long to be stung by a wasp, just so I could know for sure exactly how much it hurt — so that I could stop bloody worrying about how much it might hurt to be stung by a wasp. I do feel a little the same about needing the loo while running. It was a momentous day when, about three months into my training, I was on a cold, uphill run through Kilburn cemetery when it hit me that I was going to need a bathroom long before I was home. Beloved Kilburn cemetery, which I found so uplifting, so inspiring, such a wonderful place to run. I simply could not shit there. But for at least ten minutes I did think I was going to.

My brain was whizzing. I ran a finger around the elastic of my jogging bottoms. Could I get them down with one hand? Or would I have to put my iPod in my mouth? And my keys in my hair? I would have to move fast. I couldn't do it. By now every time

I hit the path a judder went straight up my legs and directly rattled my sphincter. I could not last much longer. Was it a bigger risk to walk and thus delay my arrival somewhere more suitable, or to run and keep the judders going? I went for a sort of tiptoe-run, as if silent footfall would con my arse into containing itself that little bit longer. I turned and crossed the top of Kilburn High Road, realising it was only five or ten minutes to home, and that it was all downhill. A good thing for my aching legs. But not even that convinced me I was going to make it. The potential horror of knowing that I had crouched beside a noble Victorian artisan's grave was now replaced with the grim vision of me running down Kilburn High Road smelling like a sewer.

Suddenly time sped up. I ceased to think of anything but the most basic survival. Like a bouncy Bear Grylls I spotted a pub on my side of the road and knew it was my only hope. There was no time left for me to fret about the fact that I had been scared of that pub and everyone I'd ever seen going in or coming out of it for three years. I made a sort of martial arts move, chopping across the wire of my headphones so that the ear buds pinged out as I entered the pub. Still moving at quite a canter I kept my eyes forward to the back of the venue and whipped straight past the barman, who was standing alone polishing a pint glass with a dishcloth.

'I need to use your bathroom, I will explain in a minute!' I yelled as I whizzed by, iPod wires windmilling behind me. Within seconds I was on the loo, stomach gurgling with relief. The heat of the building mixed with the crippling shame of my dramatic entrance meant that I was now puce, even by my own already ruddy standards. I took a deep breath, tried to run a hand through my hair, sticky with sweat. Mercifully, as I exited, the barman was now deep in conversation with a customer and I was able to give an airy wave and a cheery, 'Thank you *so* much, you're incredibly kind!' before bolting for the door.

As I headed home, running faster than I possibly ever had, a thought struck me. Being able to run was actually useful. Not just for raising money for charity or for losing enough weight to fit into a dress you thought you never would. But for getting somewhere fast. My legs seemed to be gobbling up the pavement as I headed out of that shady pub I had been so scared of for so long, but that day I could have outrun anyone in that building. I was high on the realisation for hours afterwards, as well as feeling huge relief at having made it to the bathroom at all.

* * *

With the clarity that hindsight affords I can see that my father had told me pretty much all of what I eventually worked out for myself in the first couple of months of my new running existence. Up to and including bathroom anxieties. But I didn't listen. I would see him open his mouth and hear words coming out of it, but before any of those words reached me I would launch into my own, 'Just because you have done this doesn't mean that I can't do it, I'm in my thirties now, you're not the boss of me, I will find out this information for myself because I am a strong, powerful and independent woman and times have changed since this was YOUR thing,' speech.

As I discovered when I eventually did turn back to him for help, the taste of swallowed pride is not dissimilar to that of lactic acid.

3

Wicking Fabric and How to Style It Out

'Don't bother just to be better than your contemporaries or predecessors. Try to be better than yourself.'

William Faulkner

'Oh, the great thing about running is that you don't need a whole load of fancy equipment. You just pop some trainers on and off you go!' they all kept saying.

But which trainers? While I was starting to appreciate my dad's somewhat Zen approach to running, there was one area where I decided his advice had been rendered almost obsolete in the twenty-five years since his marathon prime: kit. What was for my dad a hobby was now a market. It should not have surprised me, but the week that my fund-raising pack arrived from my chosen charity I realised what an industry running had become. So yet again I chose to wilfully ignore my dad's wisdom, deciding to try things my own way. His recommendation that

I buy trainers slightly too big seemed a nonsense. 'What could he know about running shoes?' I found myself muttering. 'He ran his first marathon in a pair of Dunlop Green Flash.'

For every piece of information I sought, whether it was about training plans, socks or moisturiser, there was someone trying to sell me something. I had no idea who to trust or where to turn for real objective advice. I had no idea what half of the products out there were actually for, or that there were solutions out there to niggles I'd discovered of my own. I had no idea what was actually worth buying. Even the language that was used in reviews for certain products seemed utterly alien to me.

But what is a new hobby if not a new shopping opportunity? Before long I had tops that looked good, but ruched up to above my waist the minute that I activated my hips. I had trousers with pockets apparently designed for a use I had yet to figure out, and I had a rain jacket with a tiny hole above my collarbone which continued to mystify me. Meanwhile I was still trying to leave the house with my fists full of coins, keys and an Oyster card, as well as my iPod.

As the weeks on my training plan peeled away I became increasingly obsessed by getting the right kit. Partly because I was now wearing it so often that it seemed insane not to like what I was wearing, but also because a sort of feral hunter's instinct had kicked in. As I waded across my flat, now a forest of drying Lycra, every radiator decorated with socks like an athletic Christmas tree, I continued to wonder whether these were the right products airing around me. I wanted to be more nonchalant about this. I wanted to be the sports shop equivalent of the cool girl who walks into a bar and challenges the boys to a game of pool. I wanted to be able to hold my own during kit chat with the lads. (That there were no lads for me to have kit chat with at this point did not deter me.) Yet I had become determined to find the very best kit to suit my needs and help my running mission.

At least for now there was one thing I didn't need: trainers. Or so I thought.

Things were looking good. My confidence was on the up. I could run for over an hour without praying for death, and I had learned some survival basics too. I was not going to dehydrate like a novice raver halfway around Regent's Park. I was not going to let a ten-pound note fly off across the river. I was not going to get lost between the Heath and my house. As Christmas approached I dared to let myself believe that I might — *might* — be able to see this through.

Until I did my first ten-mile run. I had been simultaneously looking forward to and dreading it. It was already well into the festive party season and I was feeling a little delicate. I was halfway through a crime novel I was spellbound by. I had fresh coffee in and someone had recently given me a box of peppermint creams which I hadn't quite finished. But the ten-mile milestone was ludicrously enormous and had to be passed.

The statistics rattled around in my head, becoming ever more mind-boggling with every spin. I was about to run ten miles for the first time in my life. Ten! And after only a few months of training. I absolutely knew that if I didn't get it done this weekend it wouldn't happen until after Christmas, and that by then it would be almost impossible.

All it says in my running diary after this run is, 'Very cold. Very windy. Very horrible.' It was the sort of Sunday that was made for lying in bed with someone you really, really fancy, feeding each other high carbohydrate foods and talking about novels which for that day you truly believe are meant for you and you alone. Instead I was wearing a selection of ugly, garish clothes, including a pair of fleece gloves I had been lent the previous

Christmas by my sister, and my same old tatty trainers.

It had to be done. It had to be done. It had to be done.

I set off down Maida Vale with the list of relevant street names scribbled on the back of my hand. It chafed with cold every time I peeled the glove back to check I was going the right way. I crossed the canal, headed down through Kensington and turned into Hyde Park. It was bleak, grey, almost deserted. A few old men were resentfully walking the small dogs of wives who had remained indoors. A lonely-looking father pushed a sleeping baby round and round the pond as I ran in the opposite direction. Another runner, a young guy, flashed past me and vanished into the distance down a path near the bandstand.

My ears were raw with cold. I took the glove off one hand and tried to fit my fist in my mouth just to warm it up. I wiped my bare palm across my upper lip and realised that my sweat had frozen into little salt crystals across my face. I was miserable. I headed up out of the park by Queensway and the road started to incline slightly. Every time my foot hit the pavement it was starting to hurt more and more. It felt as if the pads of my feet were entirely flat, leaving me running on near bone. I began to wince with almost every pace. My toes were the only part of my body that felt hot; now they were almost radiating. I'd never experienced this before, apart from perhaps the pain of slamming my thumb in the car door as a wriggling child. The practicalities of what I was trying to do seemed to no longer stack up. If there was so much pain in ten miles, what would twenty-six feel like? I was barely running now, just trudging along, muttering 'keep going keep going keep going' to myself, as condensation poured from my mouth.

I was two and a half miles from home — nearly there. Six months before that I couldn't even have run two and a half miles. Being 'nearly there' was an enormous feat in itself. This thought alone propelled me onwards, despite my throbbing feet. Eventually, tearfully, I made it home. My hand, now clawlike with cold, took over a minute to unlock the front door. I made myself a bowl of pasta, had a long bath, finished my book and only then looked at my feet. They seemed normal, if a little rosy. Two of my toes were very tender, like a bruised steak. It wasn't until I swung my feet out of bed the next morning that I spotted two of my toenails were dark blue.

The simplest description is that my toes

looked as if they had been hit with a hammer, cartoon-style. I didn't understand it at all, for they had not been hit by a hammer, they had simply been for a long run. I had not run on any different or unusual road surfaces. In fact I had made an effort to avoid running on the cement pavements I'd heard were bad news. Over the following days and weeks I watched with fascination as a fresh, new nail grew on two of my toes. Each one began beneath the existing nail, from just a couple of millimetres to a full-sized toenail, slowly pushing off what I now realised was a dead nail. It was mesmerising. After a couple of days there was no pain at all, merely intrigue. Would the old nail fall off before the new nail was fully grown? Was I always going to have twelve toenails now? Would the new nail grow back in time for me to paint my nails for spring? These questions consumed me. Until it was happening to my own feet I had always assumed that the dreaded process of a toenail falling off from running would involve the nail coming clean off one day, in a spurt of blood and gore. But no, nothing ever hurt as much as the day of the ten-mile run. I continued through the party season giving my open-toed shoes a wide berth. A few months later my new toenails were good to go.

A brief scan of the Internet suggested that I

needed some 'fresh' trainers after all. I discovered what had really happened: I had given myself two blood blisters from running in trainers too small. When you run for longer than about twenty minutes your feet start to swell up, just like they do after a night of fearless dancing in heels you swore fitted brilliantly when you bought them sober in full daylight earlier in the week. If you're adding that pressure to the constant slap of foot on unforgiving concrete pavement, and doing it for a couple of hours, you do in fact replicate the same injury as slamming your thumb in the car door. The thud thud thud of toes pressing between trainer toecap and road had been a mighty slam for me on that ten-mile run. It was time to confront my demons: I had to buy some new trainers.

But buying myself the right pair of trainers seemed about as possible for me as popping down to Denmark Street and buying myself the right Fender Stratocaster. I was clueless. All I knew I wanted was 'not too much pink and not too many reflecty bits like a cheerleader in the eighties please'. Vanity and my quest for respect stopped me from wanting shoes that looked 'fashion' but I had no idea whether I could pull off anything more professional looking. Like I say, I had no idea what I wanted. But I knew where to go. To the experts! So, enthusiastic little ponytail swishing in the rain, I headed to the London Marathon store in London's Covent Garden.

On the fascia outside the store there is a large digital clock that counts down the days, hours and minutes to the next London Marathon. I had worked in Covent Garden for years and at most had given it an occasional glance. I'd had the odd laugh at the earnest expressions of the men within (for they were always men) as I swerved past on the way to a post-work cocktail. Now, I needed that store. I needed it urgently.

It seemed best to push aside my quibbles about the store looking very much like one in which a woman had never set foot, and I told myself that now I was a runner I would be accepted by the staff as 'one of them'. I expected a warm welcome, a kindly listening ear for my queries, perhaps to be addressed in the manner of a colleague or at the very least a like-minded spirit.

As I tripped down Long Acre, the street where the shop resides, my nerve suddenly started to fade. The digital numbers flickered above the doorway, counting down even as I ambled up the street towards it. The numbers of days until the marathon suddenly seemed very few indeed. Niggles and anxieties I had started to leave behind found themselves wriggling back in. By the time I crossed the store's threshold my jaunty gait — which had been powered by enthusiasm and curiosity one hundred metres previously — was all but gone. The glass doors clanged behind me and two men looked up to stare at me as if I were the newest cowboy in a particularly choosy saloon. These weren't the kind-hearted fellow runners I had been hoping to encounter; they looked as if they were testing me. With my one last remaining ounce of dignity I decided to front it out.

First of all I nodded to them casually. 'Hi,' I mumbled. I edged over to the clothing, circling my eventual target gently. I picked up a couple of tops, ran their curious slithery fabric between my fingers. I replaced them on the rack. Then some running bottoms. I held a pair up to my waist, then hurriedly hung them back up again on seeing that they would no more fit me than an elephant. The younger of the two men approached me. He was wearing sports kit and a cap, and looked as if he was genuinely athletic rather than just dressing for a DVD night in. His gait was confident; he knew he knew his stuff. And he seemed to know I didn't.

'Can I help you?' he asked, as if he wasn't convinced he could.

'Yes, actually, I am looking for a pair of trainers.' A dramatic pause. I looked up and stared him in the eye. 'Because I am running the London Marathon.'

I awaited the gasps of admiration. Or at least a grunt of camaraderie. Nothing. Not even a shrug. It dawned on me that perhaps he dealt with chumps like me every day.

'If you're going to buy trainers you're going to need to be measured and we only do that by appointment and we don't have an appointment for a few weeks.' He seemed to just want shot of me. Luckily I had thought of this.

'It's OK, I know what size I am.'

'It really doesn't work like that.' He had not maintained eye contact. I was starting to sweat. I felt a dark telltale line start to appear down the back of my T-shirt. I pulled at it frantically.

'How does it work? I know my shoe size and I need some trainers.' This young chap wasn't going to get the better of me. I had money to spend and I was determined to spend it.

'Well, you'll need to run on our @£$@£ machine and then we need to look at your gait and analyse the data and then @!$£^ and in case of pronation pfftng.'

Meaningless words were just flapping

around me now. I had no idea what he was saying. Stress was buzzing in my ears like a wasp in a jam jar.

'I'm sorry, could you explain that again?'

He repeated himself. He did not explain. Ennui dripped from his every word. He gestured to a scan-like running machine in the corner of the store. This wasn't going to be like the times I was taken to Start-rite to get the new school year's T-bar shoes. My T-shirt was now sticking to my ribcage front and back.

'Well,' I said with a heavy intake of breath as I tried to summon my very best Holly Golightly face. 'Thank you for your time.'

'You need to make an appointment.'

I had no intention of making an appointment here; I was scared witless, intimidated by his talk of footfall and 'pronation', and exhausted by trying to maintain the pretence that I belonged here.

'Yes, thank you, I will call in once I have spoken to my PA.' I have never had a PA. I just wanted to go home and put on my slippers. This shop needed to not have me in it any more. But I stayed for a further two minutes, occasionally lifting and examining a pair of display trainers. I tilted my head in a manner that I assumed indicated great pensiveness on my part. As if I knew what I

61

wanted, yet I had just decided not to get it today. That was very much the impression I told myself I was giving.

Perhaps it wasn't as long as two minutes, but the burning shame rendered my cheeks a post-five-miles shade of crimson and I eventually left the shop sweating and confused. Why had I felt so humiliated? How had one sneering shop assistant managed to make me feel like such an imbecile for wanting something perfectly commonplace and fundamentally sensible?

Over time the wretchedness turned to rage. How dare they patronise me? They were there to sell me a product. Yes, it was great that they had the knowledge that I clearly needed access to, but why were they obstructing my path to it? For weeks, months even, I went on thinking that buying trainers was a rite of passage, an almost mystical experience, a ritual that you had to earn the right to participate in.

This is bullshit.

Politeness is politeness in whatever context it occurs, and it is an essential business practice. I can now say with confidence that the bloke in the store was either having a very bad day, or he was just a dick. There is no excuse for being rude to a timorous first-time runner, for making them feel stupid for not knowing the correct terminology when they have approached you for help. It takes a lot of courage to go on those first few runs and either scamming or demeaning them when they are vulnerable and in need of support is unforgivable.

So I didn't buy any trainers and went bra shopping instead.[1]

∗   ∗   ∗

Finding a decent sports bra is just as important as getting a decent pair of trainers. Mercifully I worked this out sooner rather than later, thus avoiding a nipple-related equivalent to the fate that befell my dearly departed toenails. Wearing the right bra is essential regardless of your size, as there are no muscles supporting your knockers no matter how big or small they are. If, like me, you are a cartoonish size 30FF, you are going to need some hardcore scaffolding.

The good news is that — despite what I convinced myself that one time I ran to catch a Tube while wearing a particularly diaphanous blouse — there *are* some products that

---

[1] Should you need trainers and find yourself consumed by unfamiliar shopping terrors, my guide for you is on page 272.

can all but stop your boobs in their tracks for hours at a time. And these products don't have to be bizarre combinations of sports and 'normal' bras worn over each other, as I have heard some women prefer just for running. I have lost count of the number of times women have breezily told me that they 'can't run' because of their boobs. For all that I love my boobs they are wilful and curious, always seeking a new direction to bounce around in and ever keen to seek attention on the Brighton seafront where I can least deal with the stares. But even the most unruly breasts can be contained. Yes, they can.

During my illustrious half-hearted yoga and listless gym attendance years I don't remember what sports bras I wore, but they were as primitive as they were attention-grabbing. In short they were insufficient. It was only the relaunch of the Shock Absorber in 2000 that persuaded me I could take on any sort of long-term exercise without taking someone's eye out.

I can't presume to speak for women with smaller bra sizes than me, but the problems thrown up by trying to run with a fabulous but unsupported rack are manifold. Because even when you lose a little bit of weight, thus decreasing the general body wobble that you may have started out with, your boobs will still be there. And if you do lose a few pounds they start to look even more *there*. Which can be a problem. Boobs are magnificent; you can rest cups of tea on them, feed your children with them, bring joy to mankind with them, so it really is more than a small shame when something so practical starts to feel like a burden. No one should be burdened by their knockers.

It is distressing to be exhausted at the end of a run, experiencing the weakness of doubt that you'll ever make it, only to be put off your stride even more by a grotty old man staring at your boobs as if he'd found some long-forgotten Woodbines under a sofa cushion. It is humiliating to see teenaged boys or even children snigger and whisper as you pass, when you know you'd command their respect in any other environment. It is cringeworthy to see a girlfriend catch her boyfriend copping a quick look when you have done nothing to provoke it. And it is frankly disconcerting to be running along the seafront towards two handsome men, holding hands, clearly a couple, yet both staring at your untamed breasts.

Visuals aside, the worst thing about running with big boobs and the wrong bra is the feeling that you're doing actual harm to your boobs. That feeling turns out not to be misguided. I have had more than one physiotherapist tell me that most women do more harm to their body while running in the wrong bra than in the wrong shoes. Terrifyingly, when you run, breasts don't just do the up-and-down bounce that you'd imagine in a cartoon, but they make a figure-of-eight movement. So while you might think that stopping simple bounce is enough, sports bras have to work even harder than that. The real risk of running around letting your bosom turn into a maths project is to your Cooper's ligaments. Named in the 1840s after Astley Cooper, an anatomist from Norfolk (whose father was, unsurprisingly, a clergyman), these ligaments are what protect the 'structural integrity' of the breast. Breast tissue is heavier than the fat which surrounds it, so these suspensory ligaments keep the tissue from sagging entirely or becoming one megaboob. It's best to look after them, as it is understood that once they are gone they are gone.

Then there's the chafing. A bra that is even slightly ill fitting will be unbearable after five miles, and that's before you've allowed for the abrasive qualities of rain and sweat. A small eyelet or hook coming undone can feel like someone jabbing a knitting needle in your back, and the slightest unravelling at a seam can be a disaster in saggyness.

A quarter of women wear a sports bra that doesn't fit them, and those are the ones wearing a sports bra at all. The reason most women give for not being properly measured for bra size is that they will find it embarrassing. Having suffered the humiliation of trying to buy something for my feet, I was more than a little trepidatious about attempting the same for my breasts, but boob-wise I have never been met with anything other than excellent customer service. Sweatshop stores have a specialist sports bra-fitting service staffed entirely by women who have been fully trained, as has Bravissimo, which sells all sorts of bras and is exemplary in knowing how to handle a woman who has reached the point of unmanageability with her boobs. Their staff go to something called the Boob Academy, which is an academy I can get on board with.

Having been there before, I was relatively confident about heading to Bravissimo, where I had an illustrious history of turning up and announcing that I needed help before capable yet glamorous women stared at my cleavage and sorted me out. The prospect of going to a specialist sports outfitter and trying on a random series of boxed sports bras while men stood three metres away discussing wicking fabric was out of the question. Given that you can almost definitely burn up to 300 calories in the act of just getting into a sports bra, this is an endeavour that needs to be undertaken in a calm, restful environment. Eventually I was fitted with something that fitted.

The first time I went for a run in my Shock Absorber bra was life changing. It felt like home. I am in no way exaggerating when I say that it changed not just my approach to running, but my entire outlook on what I might actually be capable of. I was snugly bound in a manner not dissimilar to that of Judy Garland in her little blue and white pinafore in *The Wizard of Oz*. My boobs were pressed to my chest in an inescapable manner, but unlike with the bra I had previously been wearing for running they were not pushed up under my chin. And I was free from that repulsive splayed effect that can only be described as 'what you might see if I were lying on a glass table and you were lying beneath it'.

As I headed out in my new bra I felt as if my legs and feet were finally free to create momentum that might push me forwards, rather than just engineer propulsion to encourage my boobs into ever more exciting formations. Similarly my arms were at last available to be used for propelling my body in the right direction, rather than being on standby as emergency dignity shields. It was liberation like I had never known.

My devotion to the bra is such that when my first one reached the end of its life — after what I estimated was over 250 miles of running, I took it apart to see how it was made. It was comprised of seventy-two parts. Seventy-two! Hooks, eyelets, slings within slings and huge, padded arm straps. Each one is a work of art, available for around thirty pounds, and I still mourn the demise of my original one. Shock Absorber bras are the results of considerable research, begun in 1994 and updated recently, and I remain slightly obsessed with them as they represent such a huge milestone in the development of my running.

My gleeful bra-based liberty was not without its woes though. There is one element to sports bra wearing that I had to work out for myself: sweat is really, really itchy. If you think of the satisfyingly crunchy granules that constitute a salt scrub and then the stinging pain that accidentally rubbing some on a recently shaved leg incurs, you will get an idea of the pain that can be inflicted on a pair of boobs unprepared for running. If you're running for over an hour, either on a sunny day or under some nice warm layers, you will create little gullies of sweat in all sorts of unexpected crevices. Then the sweat will dry in salty patterns. And then the tiny granules of salt will rub.

For the first few runs I did prior to true bra enlightenment I thought that the stinging was some sort of allergy to the fabric my bras were made of. I would collapse at home, panting, and hurl the bra from me as fast as I could, shrieking about how free I felt. Then for two or three days I would have a tiny ring of pinprick-sized blisters around my ribcage and over my shoulders where the bra had been working the hardest. After a while five or six small scars appeared, creating the impression I had a nasty taste for self-harm.

Over time I have learned that the double whammy of a well-fitting bra with a nice dollop of Vaseline underneath is the answer. As for those scars, I used to be terribly self-conscious about them, but now I am of the opinion that there is enough else in the area to distract from them, and if that doesn't work I choose not to care. They're battle wounds, they're part of me. They are a minuscule price to pay for the thousands of pounds that I have raised to help those in actual pain.

My boobs were now part of the team, working with me not against me. But in truth they weren't going to see much action unless I tackled the gruesome problem of new trainers.

My first horrendous experience at the Marathon store might have put me off indefinitely had it not been for a training day organised by London Marathon that my brother dragged me to just a few weeks later. (It is held every year — I cannot recommend it enough.) There were a series of lectures on pacing, training, injury and nutrition in a university hall; it was also the first time I had actually seen other potential runners. I was terrified at the prospect of viewing them all in an enclosed space, lithe and confident.

The reality could not have been further from the truth. I arrived very late, freezing cold from spending half an hour trying to park my Vespa in the January wind, and finally found my brother. We sat through the morning of interesting lectures but my mind inevitably wandered and I found myself studying the faces — and bodies — around me, trying to work out what sort of a runner everyone was. At lunchtime it was revealed to my immense joy that there was a room full of specialist running-shoe fitters. The marathon sponsor was Adidas so there was not a huge amount of choice but the staff there that day were of a very different breed from those at the London Marathon store. I was asked to take off my trainers and run across a sensor, then I returned to where the assistant was standing and he showed me on a large screen the way my feet fell. There, in flaring red, were the exact spots that had hurt so much on that dastardly ten-mile run. It was gently pointed out to me that for the last three months I had been running in trainers that were almost threadbare. No wonder it felt as if the pads of my feet were worn flat. They were. And as for my toes, in trainers that were half a size too small they didn't stand a chance. I was gently advised that for long-distance running one is advised to buy running shoes half a size too big to allow for the way your feet will grow during runs, and to leave them a little space to breathe. I sat down and waited for my brother to come back from his fitting. He reappeared twenty minutes later with a grin. He'd been told he'd been making all the same mistakes as me.

At the end of the day we both left the training day with running shoes that fitted properly for the purpose we were intending to use them. Not everyone needs to get measured immediately, or to make as great an emotional odyssey out of the experience as I did. But if you do end up running more than every now and again, you do need to buy sensibly. Those Adidas that I bought were perfect, my feet felt like Mariah Carey's must when she steps into bed each night. And I love them for what I achieved in them. Today they are in a state of terminal filth and I'd be repulsed to wear them again. They sit in my parents' garage, driving my mother mad on a regular basis, but I know they're there, and I like knowing that they are there.

Once the clouds of my trainer stress had parted it seemed obvious that the entire university hall was filled with people as desperate as I was to discover that they were not alone — that they weren't the slowest or the fattest or the one with the least information. We were all in it together; I was awash with relief. When I expressed this to my brother he agreed heartily before adding, 'But it's not as if we don't know anyone who has run a marathon.' I frowned, confused, before I remembered: my dad. I thought of him that first time in his Green Flash. He had worn through the soles by the end of the race, but I don't recall ever having heard him complain about it.

With the twin pillars of trainers and a bra in place I moved on to socks. Getting a decent pair is an absolute must. How complicated can socks get? was my initial response to flipping past page after page of sock advertisements in various running magazines. Then I went for a few runs in the rain in regular socks and experienced the pain of a chafing sock which has got wet and then dried against my instep. It was these raw weekends that persuaded me to invest in some double-lined sports socks. Effectively two socks attached to each other in some sort of never-ending mega-sock, they remove the friction from your feet, ensuring that any necessary rubbing goes on between the two layers of fabric rather than fabric against skin. A revolution! And don't get me started on compression socks, something I thought was a fad until I ran a marathon, had thunderingly aching legs and discovered the sweet sweet relief that wearing them brings. They feel like leg hugs, comforting and warming in equal measure, as if you have your feet up, even when you don't. I now wear them to gigs. They did me proud when I went to see Richard Hawley at the Kentish Town Forum and became delirious with lust. In hindsight I am certain that perhaps they were the only thing that kept me standing.

Once socks had given me the confidence to swagger around a sports shop asking for what I needed I was free to experiment with buying all sorts of other products, gradually assessing the weird and wonderful world of sportswear design while testing the boundaries of what I might feel comfortable running in. I was intrigued by how I could juggle everything I needed for the longer runs. For months I diligently left the house with a 500ml bottle of water only to return home under an hour later with it unopened. You simply don't always need it. Unless it's a very hot day you will be fine for about an hour as long as you've had a good couple of glasses before you leave the house.

For those longer runs there is a variety of options, from the ergonomically pleasing 500ml bottles with a hand-shaped hole in them, which ensure that your grip is not wide enough to start aching after an hour, to the high-tech backpack-style devices that carry a couple of litres, feeding a straw in your mouth when you need it. A good friend told me years later than when she undertook her longer runs she left small water bottles at the foot of trees she would pass, and drank them as she went. For me, the simplest solution always ended up making sure that I would pass either friends who I had checked would be at home with a pint glass of water near the front door, or cafes who knew my face.

But I didn't know this then. In those early days when I would continually obsess over the potential disasters that could befall me on anything longer than a 5k run (being hit by a car, passing out with exhaustion, becoming delirious with dehydration, crapping myself in the gutter, et cetera), I continued to leave the house with keys, cash for a cab, an Oyster card, iPod, water and on occasion various other bits and pieces. I'd get home with a sodden fiver and the imprint of my front door key on my palm where it had been pressed up against the water bottle. These days I take just keys and iPhone in my hand, having lost patience with those armband holders long ago. They always seemed to slip down to my wrist within three miles. I'm glad I made those early adventures into the world of kit, though I've changed my mind about a lot of it since.

One thing I have remained steadfast on is that I will probably never wear shorts to run in. I'm just not sure I will ever be able to face the twin horrors of having to see my own raw thighs looming towards me every time I take a step. They are chunky at the best of times and when I've been running for more than about ten minutes they tend to turn a colour that even a diplomat would have to describe as 'corned beef'. Add to that the uncomfortable sensation that 'loose' legs make as they hit the ground and it's all too much jiggling for me. I stick firmly to capri-length leggings for most of the year and have a couple of pairs of long running 'tights' for winter to prevent red raw ankles. I even have a pair of heavenly thermal lined running tights for winter, much to the disapproval of my brother, who is insane enough to run in shorts all year round.

The only problem to be solved once committed to running in tight leggings is that of knickers. Big, sporty, Caesarean height, a thong like a cheese wire — the list of available options is again almost infinite. I tried large, specifically sporty branded types first, but was left dispirited by the enormous dent that the seam — even from seamless ones — left beneath my running tights. The thong lasted no longer than two runs: it is impossible to get further than three miles looking and feeling so very startled. The solution I found is simple but effective: I no longer wear knickers for running. It's just another, unnecessary layer beneath a probably far superior layer of wicking fabric. There we have it.

At first I assumed that my legs would get too hot in tight capri pants year round, but in the right fabric they pose no problem. To my eternal joy I finally worked out what wicking fabric is. Rather than simply being what my mother describes as 'that disgusting slithery stuff' it is in fact a highly technical fabric that moves moisture away from the body and towards the upper surface so as to dry quickly.

When I first envisaged myself running I saw myself as Jodie Foster's Clarice Starling in the opening scenes of *Silence of the Lambs*. So strong, so focused, so proud. She is utterly confident, completely single-minded about her training run across a terrifying assault course. At one point she even runs past a tree with the sign 'HURT AGONY PAIN LOVE IT' stapled to it. She doesn't care what she looks like; she has shit to do and she is going to get it done. And yet . . . she is wearing a phenomenally impractical outfit. She is in a heavy cotton sweatshirt and tracksuit bottoms and is drenched in sweat. The top is sticking to both her chest and back and looks almost painfully heavy. She is summoned by a colleague and heads inside past a room full of people dressed in khaki faffing around with guns and then gets into a lift. All in the heavy, damp cotton. That wind-wafted wet fabric must have got incredibly cold the minute she stopped running and it bothers me whenever I think of the poor woman in that meeting. For years that scene was my running inspiration, yet now I am unable to watch the first hour of that film without worrying about whether she is shivering from the horrors of Hannibal Lecter or whether she has (arguably inevitably) caught a dreadful chill.

Mercifully fabrics these days have eradicated such issues. While modern running tops might seem oddly slithery when you're stroking them in the comfort of your wool jumper in a well-lit shop, they feel like an entirely different prospect once you're up and running on a sunny day, entirely unbothered by sweat stains or fabric clinging to your chest. Similarly, light-reflective patches on sleeves, necklines and along the edges of calves and thighs are not there, as I initially suspected, as ridiculous splashes of flashing bravado, but to potentially save your life on a dark winter's evening. I thought it was a bit of cynical branding until my brother took a picture of me in a running jacket and I realised that under his camera's flash I was actually as visible as a pushy extra in the sci-fi flick *Tron*.

In those early days my instinct was always to buy and wear clothes as baggy as possible, eager to conceal as much of my amateur blubber as I possibly could. I quickly realised how futile this is. Running clothes are not tight because retailers want you to be exposed, as I had assumed when I started trying these things on. They are just easier to run in. I have got my arm, my watch bezel or my headphone cable tangled in loose folds of flapping fabric enough times to know that this can be a disaster if a gust of wind sends things flying in your face as you approach a traffic junction, another runner or just a new lamp-post at speed. And, well, smaller clothes are just less fabric to carry around with you, or have rubbing against your shoulders, hips or ribcage as you battle through the rain on a stormy day. I am in no way suggesting than an early-Britney crop top look is the ideal for every runner, but we don't need to skulk around in a T-shirt that our husband or brother would no longer deign to sleep in.

I would frequently stand in a changing room, heart racing and hair damp with sweat, muttering darkly about why all these clothes were 'clearly designed for skinny women who are already fit'. I would wail about it incessantly to anyone who would listen, but the fact is indisputable: there is something out there for everyone. I have hunted for 'skorts' with friends who have recently had babies, discovered tiny zips and pockets that are designed to be exactly the same size as an Oyster card or a spare tampon. That hole at my clavicle on my top — it turned out to be for my headphone cable.

No one ever designed running kit to make you feel bad. In fact a lot of companies went into it specifically because the sports clothes already on the market did that in spades. The team at Sweaty Betty, led by the formidable Tamara Hill-Norton, are all women. They design the entire range at their workshop in Fulham, where mood boards and fabric ideas plaster the walls. Three quarters of them are runners, most of whom run marathons, and Tamara herself is a triathlon devotee. Their products don't always make it to the stores until they have been tested by their retail director, who does the longest runs and therefore knows how badly an ill-placed seam can irritate. They also go on buying trips to Italy to choose fabrics and colours that women might consider being seen in while sweating and struggling. Because why should we look like crap just because we're trying hard? I don't believe we should. Increasingly sports brands are realising that for as long as exercise is presented to us as a vile must-do to be fitted in between earning a living and maintaining relationships, we're going to resist it. Next time you waver at the threshold of a sports shop don't think of it as buying clothes to exercise in, but approach it as getting some kit to make your body as happy and joyful as possible. It doesn't matter if nothing matches or it gets ripped or splattered in mud, just enjoy wearing it and let your body have some fun. You should not have to choose between being a runner and being yourself.

If there still isn't anything you can find that you'd like to wear just approach the brands themselves. They're all on Twitter and @NikeSupport is already quite familiar with my steady stream of helpful suggestions and daft queries. Years before I was a runner I was randomly selected to take part in some market research for Adidas and I was stunned by the importance that they put on our emotional attachment to our sportswear. They want to know what we think; they pay people a fortune to try and figure it out. So if you have an idea, let them know.

4

We Are Family

'It is a wise father that knows his own child.

William Shakespeare'

It was only now, several months after I had started running, that I realised it was time to start listening to my dad. I barely realised that the process of paying him more attention was already well under way. It began with the flashbacks.

I had always loved and respected my father, but he's not one of life's big chatters. Apart from family and his military career, I knew little about what made him tick. Far from a cold man he is simply very self-contained — and used to a home filled with a wife and two daughters who could marathon at chatting itself, leaving him and his son for dust. My mother is effortlessly glamorous, as well as somewhat exotic. Raised in the West Indies she came to London as a teenager and became a dancer. She is rarely not wearing lipstick. She is the kind of woman who painted her nails a fresh, specific colour before each of our births. And she made staying slim seem effortless. I never saw her sweat. In hindsight she was on the move from the moment I was awake until long after I fell asleep, a constant parade of childcare and housework. On an emotional level she can be a bit 'turned up to 11'.

Adolescence saw my body change to emulate her curves and I relished it. She was the epitome of grown-up elegance and I would stare up from my seat on the carpet behind her, mesmerised at her putting on her make-up. Or I would perch, enthralled, on the edge of the bed to watch her choosing clothes before going out. I aped these little rituals as I grew older, painstakingly applying the cheapest and most basic moisturiser that she finally relented to buy me. I would swoosh the entirely unnecessary cotton-wool ball loaded with unnecessary cold cream over my face, sweeping it across the area where I hoped my cheekbones would grow, desperately hoping that this would launch me into full adulthood.

Meanwhile my father seemed to become more distant, or at least more different. When I was a child he had been everything I could ask for in a father. He was endless fun in the garden, constantly inventing games, never tiring of lifting and throwing us from bike to swing and back again as we shrieked and gallivanted. He always had time and he always had energy. But once I had outgrown prancing around in the garden with him, what we had in common seemed to decrease at speed. I wanted to chat about bras and shoes, not tanks and foreign policy. As I discovered boys and developed a taste for their associated dramas it didn't seem terribly cool that my dad was a polite, charming and kind man.

As I headed into my twenties this pattern seemed fixed. I loved my father, but I didn't really know how to communicate with him. Our relationship was static. I accepted this as permanent and gave it little further thought. Until I bought a copy of *Runner's World*.

As part of my explorations into the world of running kit I had timorously bought my first copy of the magazine at a busy train station. I instantly set about reading it from cover to cover. A couple of mornings later I swung my legs out of bed, pushed myself up in a fog of sleepy limbs and immediately skidded a foot across the room on the magazine's glossy cover. I looked behind me at the creased pages and headed to the kitchen. As I closed my eyes, waiting groggily for the kettle to boil, I saw a clear image of the permanent heap of running magazines that my father kept at his bedside — on the floor. I remembered trying not to skid on them as I clambered up into their bed on a Sunday morning. I remembered one time actually skidding on them and sending a cup of coffee flying across the carpet. I remembered my mother trying to tidy them up, time and time again.

'Why must they be here in my bedroom?' 'They are so ugly!' 'I keep skidding on them!'

I smiled slowly to myself. For the first time ever I felt a tiny morsel of what it was like to be my father.

A few weeks later I tried to leave my flat, only to trip over a heap of trainers by the front door, drying on a sheet of newspaper after a particularly rainy run. An image of my mother doing the same thing at home flashed across my mind. Suddenly I could remember every crease of those mid-eighties New Balance shoes. They were the sort of trainers that forty-something men who have non-specific jobs in digital content agencies now wear to the office. Back then, however, they were my father's most prized possession. The kit of champions.

Not long after that I discovered the joy of a long, silent bath after another of my longer-than-I'd-ever-run-before training sessions. As I closed my eyes and rested my head on the back of the bath another childhood flashback appeared: my sister and I hopping outside of the family bathroom, rattling the locked door handle, desperate for our father to come out and play in the garden with us. Our mother ushering us downstairs with a stern, 'You know how tired he is after a marathon.' He ran marathons and then came home to a family of three children? Of course he did, I realised. He did it several times.

Floodgates had opened. Suddenly my childhood seemed to be undergoing a re-editing process. My father wasn't in shorts for breakfast most mornings because he dressed like one of us, but because he had just returned from a run. We played the best games in our garden because our dad was the fittest, the strongest. The downstairs bathroom was not just where my mum kept a spare bottle of perfume but also where his increasing collection of marathon medals would hang.

The next time I called home I stopped him when he did his usual, 'I'll get your mother for you . . . '

'Hang on,' I said. 'I want to ask you something. How many marathons did you do in the end?' It must have been five or six all in all, I thought to myself.

'Nineteen,' came the reply.

'Nineteen?!'

'Yes.'

'But I don't remember you doing half of them.'

'Well, I did nineteen official ones but sometimes I used to just do runs that long as well.'

'Oh my god. How, HOW?'

Five minutes later we were still having one of the longest chats we'd had for months, possibly even years. Suddenly we had a way of communicating and over the weeks that followed it became a secret language. He would call me with news of compression socks he had seen in the paper, or supplements, or training tips. We would chat about how my latest runs were going and I would ask him for advice and motivation. He would cut things out of the paper and send them to me, or save books he had found for the next time I visited home. It didn't matter that sometimes I had no real news about my fitness; it became something we always chatted about anyway, our common ground. It was now 'our thing'.

Increasingly he was the only person who kept me going on some of those long runs. The thought of how he had just got up every morning for years and done it with so little fuss that the most my mother had to complain about was slipping on a magazine. As my body began to change shape I realised that I hadn't just developed my mother's figure over the years. All that time I had thought that we were so different, my father and I. Yet the first time I saw a photograph of myself running, I could pinpoint the exact mid-eighties photograph of my father that it reminded me of.

These legs were his. It was his lungs that were powering me up hills. And it was his quiet acceptance that yes, running can be hard but that yes, it is worth it that was helping me get through the most desperate moments of my training.

Meanwhile my mother maintained a sort of detached bemusement about these develop-ments and this in turn amused me. I would come home for the weekend and spend an hour poring over maps at the kitchen table, trying to work out a great training run. She would stare across the room with the same benign lack of interest that she had displayed twenty years earlier when a new pair of New Balance trainers would arrive. My dad would order them from the States and they took weeks to arrive via the military post to whichever army base we were stationed at. The day he brought them home was always exciting. New trainers! Back then I thought that the excitement on his face was never ever matched by the grey practicality of what lay within. I smiled and remembered my mother's baffled eye roll as she picked a trainer up, ran her finger along the mouse-like suede, then returned to whatever she was doing. Somehow things had changed. These days I understood the joy of a new pair of trainers and what they represented.

In time the more I ran, and the more I cared about running, the more I realised I had in common with my father. I started making up random running queries just so I could call for a bit of a pep talk from time to time. He was becoming more than a father and more than a friend; he was becoming a genuine inspiration to me.

As the marathon training runs became longer I started doing more of them near to my parents' house in Wiltshire, the heart of Hardy country. Aside from the glorious views there were the benefits of my dad's advice along the way. We enjoyed marking out potential courses on his chaotically photocopied Ordnance Survey maps the night before, drawing the route with a highlighter pen and then folding and wrapping the paper in a plastic folder that I could carry in my palm. I'd be approaching a hill that had appeared so inviting from the comfort of a gliding car's window but was in fact at a relentless, demonic gradient when I'd see him at the side of the road with water and half a banana.

'I figured you'd be about here!' he'd say as I tearfully asked to be driven home. 'Not a chance,' he'd say, patting my back. 'I saw the way you took that hill on, you've got at least three more miles in your legs. See you later for lunch!'

It was like talking to a hellish sort of tower of confidence. There was no negotiating his faith in what I could achieve. At times infuriating, it was also powerful. It kept me going. It got me home in time for lunch.

I was also calling my brother more often, and for ever-increasingly geeky conversations: maps, routes, training schedules, lined socks and weird new food groups. We tried to understand fartlek. We giggled. By Christmas I was a proper runner. I received thermal running tights from my brother on Christmas Day and didn't break my marathon training schedule. Running was changing everything.

It wasn't just my family who saw these changes in me and my attitude to myself and others. After a lifetime of endlessly discussing feelings, having spats and indulging in gossip with my mother, sister and female friends, I recognised that I had developed a better understanding of how to communicate in a wider sense. It didn't always need to be spelled out. Sometimes time is how you spend your love. Without ever expressing my new-found closeness to them I realised that as the time I spent with my father and brother had increased, so had my confidence when dealing with men in general.

After Christmas marathon training continued, and I began to sense respect from both men and women as I talked about it more. I enjoyed having my body praised for what it could do rather than how it looked. For years I felt my male friends had seen me as a woman first and a friend second, and I had never troubled a boyfriend with my almost anti-competitive spirit. My new-found physical ease didn't merely translate to moving my arse closer to the holy grail of 'looking better in jeans' but to making the world seem smaller, more accessible on foot. It became — and remains — a delicious pleasure to stride up the left-hand side of the escalator in a Tube station, my breathing steady and the strength of my own legs powering me faster to wherever I've chosen to be. I imagine people wondering how I've done it and the answer is simple: I decided to be able to.

It wasn't just moments of passing smugness that were my treats, it was being able to have more fun with more spontaneity. I will never forget the look on my toddler godson's face as I saw him for the first time in a few weeks and picked him up like a tiny rocket ship, blasting him into the air. After months of running up hills my arms were stronger than I had realised and my enthusiastic 'Woooooosh!' was followed by my nearly shoving him through the kitchen ceiling. Our nervous laughter as we both realised I had not been prepared for what I could now do created a conspiratorial giggliness that we maintained for the rest of my visit.

As my body changed and my sense of what it was capable of started to shift I developed a more masculine side to my personality and, dare I say it, a competitive streak. I was getting to know my way around London per mile, rather than per Tube stop. I was happy to engage in sporting chat in a way that I could have done only with a heavy sense of irony before. I found the confidence to breezily wander around shops filled with fitness and sports kit.

To my surprise my new knowledge and grit didn't lead to me becoming a social outcast, but actively seemed to make people more interested in me. While women were admiring of my tenacity with the training and my ever-leaner legs, men wanted to chat. They actually seemed to want to know more about me. Not just the technical sports fabrics, but *me*. I was getting admiration, interest and kudos not just from blokes I was dating, but whom I'd known for years. My male friends were viewing me with renewed respect: She's actually going to go through with this, I could see them thinking.

In turn this new-found confidence filtered down into my relationships with female friends too. I sensed respect from them: I was sticking to my plan, I was going to get it done. In embracing my masculine side I was becoming a better woman. I found it easier to admit that I had goals, or dreams, and that it took a little tenacity to achieve them.

After a lifetime of accepting that my body was to be looked at rather than used, I was learning to appreciate what it could actually do. Food became a practicality, not merely an indulgence or a torment. The distance between food and pleasure became wider and wider as I came to associate it more with fuel. I never stopped enjoying it, but I enjoyed it differently — because it helped me, not because I had guiltily used it as a bribe to get me through bleak days or cold nights. I became proud of my strong thighs rather than frustrated by the limitations imposed by what trousers they may fit into. I didn't care that I would never be as thin as some girls. Because

I would be stronger than many. While compliments are always lovely I struggled to care when people would tell me how much weight I'd lost. 'But have you seen what I can do now?' was all I ever wanted to reply.

Somehow removing the idea of exercise simply as something to do with getting fit or reaching aesthetic perfection had made sport a very different experience for me. I was enjoying the thrill of setting goals and sticking to them, of developing a bit of mental discipline. I was able to use my old pal, my mind, to conquer what I had previously thought physically impossible. I saw that these qualities needn't be unfeminine or aggressive but were actually attractive.

It wasn't all Pollyanna-ish goals and challenges either. I cherished the simple childlike glee of shoving on weird, bright, stretchy clothes and going outside to leap around to loud music. I let my mind float off, pretending to be whichever pop or rock star I was listening to, or imagining I was running from certain peril or simply that I was winning a race I'd never entered. I chuckled inwardly as I wondered if passers-by could see me nodding to a particularly juicy bass line. My face would soften as a song appeared on my playlist that had been sent to me as part of a flirtation. I grinned as a song that reminded me of a particularly high-octane party appeared out of nowhere. I was getting little extra bursts of living out there with my music, the intensity of each emotion accelerated by the fast pumping of my blood.

My confidence, which had been battered and bruised by both romantic and career endeavours felt as if it had been given a sort of emotional Botox. Boosted from within it felt plumped up, more delicious than it had been in years. The simple fact of running around meant I saw more people, my place in the world felt a little sturdier, everything felt a little less of a catastrophe and a bit more like the natural ebb and flow of life.

My gaze began to turn outwards and running ceased to be about what others might see when they looked at me, but about what I saw when I ran. I started to find the change in the seasons more interesting than the changes in my body. It was this weight that was the heaviest I could have shed. I was no longer running simply to prove that I could finish a marathon, or to impress my dad or even to sound good on dates. I was using these runs to give me clarity and focus, to remind me of what I was capable of and to spur me on in all areas of my life. I felt unstoppable.

Until one day I had to stop.

5

Injury

'Everyone who has run knows that its most important value is in removing tension and allowing release from whatever other cares the day may bring.'

Jimmy Carter

I knew it would be a cold January run when I set out from home to Hampstead Heath. I had on my new thermal leggings and a pair of gloves. After half an hour I was coping pretty well. The tip of my nose was as ruddy as ever, but my eyes were not watering too much and my feet were surprisingly warm. For reasons I didn't fully understand it was my hips that were taking the full blast of that afternoon's icy winds. Each stride I took started to feel more like a stinging slap than the last. It had happened once or twice before, but it had been a long cold winter and I assumed that this was just a weak spot of mine.

Stopping to cross the street I tried lifting my heel up behind me and grabbing onto my foot to stretch out my hip flexors. I slapped the top of my thighs on either side, trying to get the blood circulating, anything to warm up. It was no use, the pain was getting worse. Eventually I decided that I wouldn't run as far as I had planned and headed home with only two thirds of a run completed. I had to almost drag my leg behind me home, despondent at the parade of runners sailing by me along Maida Vale.

An hour later, once I'd had a hot bath and changed, I knew my hips had warmed up properly. But the pain across the top of my right leg was still excruciating. It felt as if someone had tightened the ligaments and tendons holding me together. I wanted to stretch and stretch, but it never made anything feel any better.

I headed out to the Tube, on my way to meet a friend at the cinema. I barely made it to the station, now almost unable to lift my leg for each stride. By the time I reached the South Bank tears of pain were stinging my eyes. What had happened? I hadn't fallen or knocked myself. I hadn't knowingly sprained anything. I had no idea what could be causing me such piercing agony, and spent the length of the film shifting in my seat, longing to know if a decent rest would ease it. As the credits rolled I dreaded standing and testing my leg. The pain was even worse than I could have imagined.

Within forty-eight hours I was sitting in a physiotherapist's consulting room. I was lucky to have been recommended a decent sports physiotherapist. Josie — a dark-haired woman as tiny as she was commanding — was sympathetic and genuinely interested in what was causing my pain. Within minutes she had got me down to my pants and bra and had stuck tiny dots — the sort that usually indicate that a painting has been sold — on my shoulders, hips, elbows and the backs of my knees. Then she put me on a running machine and told me to jog, which she filmed for a few minutes. The hip pain had eased considerably by then, but still I was wincing at the prospect of this exercise.

I survived it and once I was dressed Josie rewound the footage and looked at it. Then we watched it together, her eyes hard with concentration, mine glazed with the sort of hopeful ignorance I had previously reserved for trying to spot the baby in a friend's ultrasound snapshot. Moments later she looked at me and asked, 'Have you had an accident recently which had a large impact on the left-hand side of your body?'

I had not.

' . . . And possibly a secondary impact on the right?'

Nothing rang any bells. I had been fine for

months, perhaps even a year. Sure, I often had pain in my pelvis after sitting down for long journeys and had done since long before I started running, but it seemed like a fair trade-off for a job that saw me mostly sitting at a laptop or curled in bizarre positions reading.

I looked blank. 'No, nothing.'

'Are you sure? You seem to have sustained a pretty big blow,' Josie repeated.

I racked my brains. Surely I would remember a massive blow to the left-hand side of my body.

'No, really, I'm fine.'

'OK, have you ever been in a traffic accident?' she persisted.

'Really, no, I have never been in a car crash,' I replied, as frustration at her sure-mindedness bubbled up in me.

As my mouth formed that final 'sh' the realisation hit me with a crash of its own: four years previously I had been knocked off my Vespa on Kilburn High Road by a four-by-four when it turned right without looking and drove straight into me. Sure, I had never been in a car crash. That was because I had been on a scooter. And then in the air.

As I watched the tape replay again and again suddenly every bit of pain I had felt for the last four years made sense. Josie slowed down the footage and showed me my running gait in motion, complete with all of its attendant weaknesses. At the time of the accident I had been checked over and told that bar a few ripped muscles I had sustained no serious injuries. But back then I wasn't a runner. What was now more than evident as I watched myself run on the treadmill in my pants, the little dots rising and falling in irregular patterns, was that I had been injured after all. My pelvis was not quite in the correct place; it had been knocked around by the impact of that huge car on my sitting frame. Consequently my body had adapted around that injury, growing weaker and stronger in equal measure.

My running training had made me stronger — but not symmetrically so. I had started to develop something of an imbalanced Frankenstein's monster of a body. The front of one thigh was strong but with a weak hamstring behind it. The reverse was true of the other leg, which was slightly further forward than its partner on account of my misaligned pelvis. This pattern was repeating itself across my entire body, until my front hip flexor was no longer able to pull my leg forward without excruciating pain. All because one woman in a Chelsea Tractor could not be bothered to check her wing mirrors four years ago.

I sat on the edge of Josie's consulting

couch, watching my marathon dream fade to tatters. I swallowed time and again, desperate not to cry in front of someone I had only just met. What was to be done? Could I run again? Or were all of those people who had claimed that running would 'destroy your legs' correct after all?[1]

Josie calmly talked me through what I had to do and how we were going to get it sorted. While fascinating tales of high-tech surgery would be enthralling the reality was much the same as it had been throughout this process: hard work. She told me immediately that I could not run for at least a month, until I had done exercises every day to strengthen and rebalance the muscle groups that were now working so hard against each other. Small, firm Pilates-like movements were painstakingly gone through every day — often while tied to a door handle or the back of a chair with stretchy physio banding to get the necessary resistance. Slowly, over the next few weeks, I managed to right myself. It was too late for me to be perfect in time for the marathon, but the dream was not over. I willingly submitted to whatever Josie instructed

------

[1] Don't panic as much as I did that day — there is a section on the myths and facts around running injuries on page 246.

me, secretly impressed with my pain threshold for having let me carry on as long as I had managed to.

But it wasn't the pain or the tedium of the exercises that proved to be the worst part of this experience. It was not being able to run. Under Josie's instruction I joined my local council gym for a month so that I could keep my fitness up on other machines. Anything but running. What had so recently been an activity that filled me with sheer dread was now what I longed to do more than anything else. I felt caged in the gym, I would wake having dreamt of running and in my waking hours I fretted endlessly about what would happen the next time I attempted a run. The idea that I had once been anxious about buying a pair of socks seemed ludicrous compared to my fears about having to give up running for good. Having gone from viewing my body as a tedious accessory to something genuinely useful, I now saw it as a great treasure. For six weeks I followed Josie's orders, I shunned high heels, I prayed for the best.

My body was now my friend and ally. I needed it to help me through my biggest challenge. And over these weeks I also came to see the role that my mind had in this recovery, because with running injuries it is very often the case that you don't know how recovered you are until you undertake a long run. You have to be prepared to fail, but nor can you let yourself consider that tiny window of possibility. Like a grim game of chicken I vacillated between wanting as many people as possible to know about the injury and keeping it a secret so it couldn't take hold and gain power over me.

As marathon day itself grew closer I began some tentative recovery runs. Amazingly the pain had gone. It looked as if I would still be there on the starting blocks after all. I never managed to entirely catch up with my original training plan, but I did what I could within the limited timeframe. I got through March thanks to Josie, late nights spent chatting on the London Marathon website and a steady stream of texts, emails and chats with my dad. I stretched, I fretted, I did my strengthening exercises. I watched the entire first series of *The Wire* standing with one foot tied to the bottom of a table leg. I did everything I could think of to get through, up to and including pestering everyone I knew for sponsorship, just to drive home how much I needed to get round that course. But one fact remained: the only way to truly find out if I was physically — or mentally — capable of finishing a marathon was to try and run a marathon.

6

The London Marathon

'If you are losing faith in human nature, go out and watch a marathon.'
                    Kathrine Switzer

I could not have done more to prepare for my first London Marathon, yet I have never been less prepared for anything in my life. My mental image of the 'starting blocks' was not dissimilar to that of an egg and spoon race at a school sports day: a handful of eager enthusiasts willing to give it their very best. The reality felt more like Glastonbury. I was exhausted before I even reached the starting line.

As marathon day approached my behaviour had become increasingly like a neurotic combination of Usain Bolt and Anna Pavlova. The day before, my parents and sister came up to London to cheer me and my brother along, and we all went to the local pub for a high carb lunch. I walked delicately, worried that the slightest knock could damage my chances of reaching the finish line with a misplaced bruise or sprain. I did not eat delicately and polished off a bowl of seafood pasta as if it were my death row meal. Then my sister ordered us shots of sambuca, convincing us that it would wear off long before bedtime.

When bedtime did arrive I found myself wishing there was some sambuca in the house. I walked into the sitting room before I went to bed and checked my sports bag, all packed for the next morning. My kit was laid out next to it. I had never been more awake. Perhaps it was nerves, perhaps it was my body swimming in carbohydrates. Either way I slept lightly, lying awkwardly in a variety of positions I thought would rest my muscles as much as possible, while a million worst-case scenarios played out in technicolour across my imagination.

Within seconds of my alarm sounding I was whipping up scrambled eggs at the hob with a speed and focus my military father would have been proud of. I swallowed it grimly, still full from the day before. Its relentless rubberiness reminded me of school food: necessary nutrition and nothing more. I dressed, checked my bag another six or seven times and sat on the very edge of the sofa waiting for the taxi. Twenty minutes later I was approaching Charing Cross station to meet my brother. His journey to marathon day had been considerably smoother than mine, but he had experienced just as much nervousness as I had in the final few weeks. We had shared late-night anxieties, bizarre and hitherto unfamiliar food cravings and endless tips with each other, and he had provided a steadfast level of support since day one. I could barely wait to see him. I had imagined he'd be easy to spot, a lone nerdy runner in a sea of London day-trippers and homeward-bound nightclubbers. The reality made me draw breath. The *only* passengers at Charing Cross were runners. It was a sea of tense, solitary figures in wicking fabric, each one numbered and labelled like a refugee. There was barely space for us all on the trains heading towards Greenwich, and we shuffled uncomfortably onto the carriages in an eerie silence. I assumed everyone else was an old-timer, destined for an impressive three-hour finish time and a quick fry-up before heading home. I know better now: that silence was just a result of us all thinking the same thing. Everyone was nervous, whatever their fitness or experience.

We poured out of the station at Blackheath and began the fifteen-minute walk across the grass. The weather reports had been mixed all week, predicting everything from rain and wind to sun and unicorns. But as we headed through Southeast London the air was crisp and clear. I imagined I had joined a cult that met in a secret London I never usually saw. We were marching to some sort of promised land, searching for answers from a leader we had yet to meet. It was still an hour before official start time; what would we do until then? What else did this strange pilgrimage hold for us? The answer, it turned out, was Portaloos.

We stopped at them twice, thoughts of road-side peeing looming ever larger in our terrified minds. On entering and exiting we avoided eye contact with the other runners, kindred pilgrims complicit in the same fleeting madness. When we reached the starting-line area the atmosphere became more like that of a carnival or feast day than the earlier reverence. A tannoy belted out relentless motivational music and a cheesy DJ read requests and good-luck messages. A gospel choir would not have surprised me. Half an hour later I spotted one.

There were stalls selling water and food, and the rows upon rows of luggage trucks only served to emphasise the enormous portable spectacle that we were irredeemably a part of. Now numbed by the volume of activity around me I handed over my bag with barely a second thought.

Relieved not to have missed any trains or broken any legs en route my brother and I became almost hysterical, the mood of the crowd sweeping us up in the spirit of nervous anticipation. Still nibbling on oatcakes and bananas with gritty determination we joined the hordes of runners leaning against trees doing last-minute stretches, and took silly photos of each other in our running vests. Maybe it would be fun after all, we started to tell each other, stealthily glancing around. Everyone here seems to be OK. I relaxed into the idea of spending the day in Greenwich Park, getting to know my new friends, my fellow pilgrims. Then, suddenly, we were called to the starting enclosures. Just as suddenly I desperately wanted to go home.

The volume of runners at an event as large as the London Marathon is such that you are asked to state your predicted time when you apply for a place. Six months of sweat later you are then divided into 'pens' of half-hour intervals. The fastest runners leave first so that they don't become trapped behind the nervous and the becostumed. The me that had filled in that form now seemed as foreign as the professional athletes warming up for the BBC cameras. I'd had no idea what I might be capable of; the very prospect of finishing had filled me with wide-eyed wonder. Consequently I had no recollection of what I had stated as my predicted time back in October, and it was only when we collected our race numbers that I discovered I'd gone for the slowest time possible. My brother, who had done some basic research, had not. He was due in a pen 200 metres from me. He turned and grinned at me.

'Good luck!' he said, stretching his arms out for a hug and doing his very best to mask his own nerves. 'You'll probably win!' My baby brother, heading off without me. My bottom lip wobbled.

'Have an amazing time,' I replied, trying not to look flustered by the huge number of runners flocking towards their starting enclosures. 'See you at the end — and text me when you've finished!'

I walked towards my pen, which now seemed to be entirely populated by cartoon characters and the elderly. My cheeks burned with shame as I realised that my low expectations for myself had labelled me as one of this lot. I looked around and smiled, hoping for a similarly aged face that might take pity on me and smile back. Everyone else seemed to be with someone, bonding over something. The crowd packed in around me, only serving to emphasise the aching loneliness that was suddenly washing over me. I felt something like the homesickness that I had felt as an eight-year-old at boarding school for the first time. The thought of the run no longer bothered me. But the thought of doing this alone, with nothing but my thoughts for the next few hours, was flooding me with anxiety.

Simultaneously a second problem I had never even considered was creeping up on me — my fear of crowds. I have never been to a music festival, I avoid the first day of the sales and I skulk around at the beginnings and ends of big sporting events until almost everyone has left. I have jumped fences in Hyde Park and run through the trees in the dark to avoid the drunken crowds coming out of concerts. I always, always seek to avoid my worst nightmare: being caught up in an unpredictable tsunami of humans. If possible, I will always walk rather than take a packed Tube or I'll wait until a crowd has passed, so horrified am I of being moved by a mass of bodies in a direction I can't control. I looked around those pens, occasionally bouncing on tiptoes to check on the river of people ahead, and saw that this was exactly where I was. Six months of training, most of them entirely alone, for this: the biggest crowd I had ever been part of. As I had pounded my local pavements alone, run across ox droves and through grassy valleys circling my parents' home, and even around the lanes of Tobago on holiday, I had never, ever considered that on the day there would be other runners alongside me. How had I not thought of this? How would I find my place among the bodies? How would I deal with the relentless lava flow of runners around me?

My heart hammered in my chest and I stared down at my trainers, hoping to both hide and contain the rising panic. The feet around me began their slow shuffle towards the start line. I looked up; the red 'Start' banner was still so far away that we couldn't even see it. We moved forward, the chatter rising and falling, people wishing one another luck. The pace quickened as we turned the corner and suddenly saw the arch, with its familiar clock sitting above it. The crowd began to jog, slowly, apprehensively at first. And then a real run as we crossed the mats that triggered the timer chips tied to our trainers. People around me cheered and whooped as they set off. I let out a nervous, fluttering laugh. I was running the London Marathon.

Five minutes into the first mile the crowd had eased into more of a steady pace. I was able to overtake a few people who were jogging slowly. We were heading through Greenwich, streets of smart residential houses with families outside — many still in pyjamas and dressing gowns — wishing the runners well and cheering them along as they hugged morning cups of tea to themselves. Their smiles lifted me as my heart rate levelled out and my feet began to find a regular rhythm.

Half an hour later my attitude to the crowd was shifting. I felt dependent on the steady thud of others' feet as we curled gently round corners as one, our pulses quickening in unison as we headed up the occasional inclines. I looked around me and started to recognise faces, their numbers and names from earlier in the day. We were all in it together. We were like a family now. I would not complete this alone after all. A surge of confidence bubbled up in me and I began grinning and waving at the spectators. I felt like a rock star, as though an occasional glance from me could inspire a watching child to a lifetime of athletic prowess. *Yes! You can be whoever you want to be!* I felt like shrieking it to each and every one of them as I sailed past, legs strong and heart pumping.

We turned another corner and there was another line of children with their hands outstretched, hoping to catch high fives from the passing competitors. Largely they went ignored as the crowd was still shuffling for positions, teddy bears jostling among Smurfs for superiority on the road. Occasionally someone would run by and slap their hands, leaving a little ripple of grinning children behind them. I decided I'd be one of them. I spotted a gap in the sea of people and took a couple of steps towards the edge of the road, stretching out my arm. My yearning for a bit of human contact and these small hands seemed like the perfect exchange of comfort for acknowledgement.

I leant forwards and reached out for one of the hands, continuing to run as I grinned down at the child. I felt the ground rushing up towards me. Before I could work out what was happening it struck my left hip and a rush of heat seared across my thigh as I skidded along the road. I had not spotted the kerb; in reaching for those hands I had lost my footing and fallen, my legs a rag-doll jumble around me. I stared at the tarmac, sweating under the disappointed gaze of the children, painfully aware of the inconvenience I was causing to other runners as they had to step around me. Gasping I sprang up, pushed my hair back off my face and carried on running.

I longed for the debilitating shame of

tripping and falling alone, when all that is left for you to do is to glare at the guilty pavement. I had done that many times before and almost developed a technique for coping with it. This time the shame was a hundred times worse, surrounded as I was by an audience. Their pitying gasps, their shaking heads, their angry shuffles past.

The price of vanity, I could feel them thinking. Only a first-timer would do that.

Soon the pain of embarrassment was replaced by a rush of physical pain. Each time my right thigh rose towards me I saw that my running tights were shredded. I was grazed and bruised from shoulder to elbow to knuckles, as well as the length of my thigh, where flecks of lacerated Lycra were now embedded. The blood from my leg was starting to drip downwards and my pelvis was giving its familiar dull ache.

Sweat met blood met fabric in dappled crops of stinging. As the blood dried each extension of my thigh caused it to crackle and split, and a fresh smattering of pain would work its way across me. I knew I had to get some antiseptic on the grazes and a mile later I spotted a St John's Ambulance tent. I ran off the main road and into the tent. I arrived, panting, unused to a world where I stood still and others moved. A reassuring-looking elderly lady with a whipped-cream topping of a hairdo looked up and smiled at me.

'Hello, dear. Our first customer of the day! What seems to be the problem?' she asked with all the urgency of a woman judging a Victoria sponge at a village fete. The feet passing outside the tent made a constant rumble as all the runners I had overtaken in the last hour steadily passed me. 'Oh dear, that's a nasty graze isn't it?' Her tone was one of a kindly grandmother.

'I'm running a race!' I wanted to shout. 'Help me, I need to get back there.' One of the Smurfs passed the tent's entrance as it flapped open in the breeze.

'Pam, do we have any antiseptic wipes?'

My heart was struggling to know what to do. Beat slower because of standing still or beat faster in panic at my new friend's apparent lack of urgency.

'Oooh, I think they're in the holdall June just brought in,' came the reply.

'Now, dear, can you just fill in this form so they know what we've done with you?'

'I just wanted you to check there was no grit in my grazes really.'

'I understand, dear, now what's your date of birth?'

'The fourteenth of — '

'Oh, now isn't that lovely eye make-up,

116

June? So nice that the young lady's made an effort for the big day . . . '

I wanted to be angry, but I was so relieved that someone was taking care of me. I wanted to be running, but there was no chance of that for another few minutes at least.

'Apparently the weather's going to turn in a bit, but you wouldn't believe it looking at the sky, would you?'

I winced. I'll never know if it was the pain of her dabbing at the grazes or the sight of two men dressed as a rhinoceros stomp past the tent. It had taken me three minutes to get past them half an hour ago.

Eventually June's friend deemed me fit to run. I begged for some anti-inflammatory pills for the bruising but they were firm that they were not allowed to give me any. I left the tent and my twelve minutes of unscheduled static contemplation behind me. Rejoining the throng was harder than starting at the beginning of the race. I had been wrenched in the wrong direction; all my confidence had evaporated and I was surrounded by a gaggle of fancy-dress runners, valiant old folk and others barely doing more than a walk. I loved these guys, I knew I could happily spend the next five hours with them and trundle to the finish declaring myself injured. But I knew how hard I had trained. And I knew my injuries were probably only superficial. I had to make a decision: run around them in order to regain a steady pace getting a few miles under my belt, or run treacle-slowly, expending no energy on dodging rhinos, but letting the marathon continue almost infinitely. To make matters worse, the thud of pain was now reappearing and it was only going to get worse.

I chose the former, and I didn't enjoy a second of it. Instead of running in a straight line I was now effectively running twice as fast and twice as far as everyone around me. I wove across the road, shimmying between women chatting about their grandchildren, ducking beneath whacky headgear and dodging around Mr Men. Every twist and shimmy created blooms of pain in my joints while I seemed to go nowhere. The heavens finally opened, just as they had been promising. I was glad of the wet, as it hid the tears I shed for three miles. Plodding through the rain my trainers swelled and my heart felt as heavy as my now sodden ponytail. I was playing out different excuses in my mind, performing imaginary role plays of how I'd explain to friends and family that I'd had to give up on the marathon halfway because of some grazes and sprains.

This reverie had now become almost

enjoyable, the masochism of my new determination to fail consuming me. My phone buzzed with a text from my father. They were nearby, less than a mile away, waiting to cheer me on up Jamaica Road, around mile eleven. My father, my mother and my sister. I refreshed my master plan. I would keep going at least until I had seen them; it would be rude to deprive them of the chance to see me running after waiting all that time. Then I would decide whether to abandon the mission. As I approached their location I started to crane my neck, hoping to spot one of them in the thick ropes of crowd, maybe catch a smile before running by. No need. I heard my mother's voice rise like a lark above the rest of the uniform cheering.

'COME ON MY DARLING GIRL YOU ARE DOING SO WELL, NOT TOO FAR BEHIND YOUR BROTHER! KEEP GOING YOU STRONG STRONG THING AND MAYBE YOU'LL CATCH HIM AND SHOW THOSE BOYS WHAT WE'RE MADE OF!'

'I've fallen!' I replied, pointing to my shredded leggings.

'KEEP GOING YOU LAUGH IN THE FACE OF PAIN!' was the reply I received, amidst further whooping from the three of them.

A nearby mother looked with concern at

her baby, trying to edge the buggy away from my family's combined raucousness. I shrieked, as did my sister as soon as she saw me, and they all burst into cheering, waving and clapping. Their fellow onlookers understood that a loved one had been spotted and joined in with the yelling. A ripple of goodwill passed through them and made its way towards me and my neighbouring runners. Someone nearby slapped me on the back as I passed them, wiping my eyes.

The difference having supporters makes when you're running a public event is incalculable, whether you know them or not. It is never, ever unwelcome. (Unless, perhaps, they're enjoying a fag with their roadside pint and blowing the smoke into the runners' faces.) Those few seconds of hearing people shout your name, showing that they're prepared to stand at the side of a road to cheer you on, demonstrating that they have faith you'll make it and that they'll still be there for you even if you don't, can keep a lonely runner going for miles. I was especially buoyed up by the sight of my family wailing encouragement at me and it became infectious among the other runners too.

As we turned along the river and approached Tower Bridge and the thirteen-mile mark I felt part of a communal effort once again. The mass of runners hugged me as the road narrowed and the towers loomed into sight. Bands and cheering grew louder. For the second time since setting off the powerful feeling of sharing a tough job seemed to spur us runners on and we were all grinning. We felt like superheroes as we crossed the river, a bout of welcome sunshine drying us out and making us giddy with excitement. I grinned at a Captain Caveman waving his plastic club at the spectators and roaring. He caught my eye and grinned back. My earlier resentment of the slower runners now felt like a sort of security. Once again I felt that we were in it together. We were doing it for each other. And we were halfway! Maybe I could do it after all, and maybe, *maybe* it was worth it.

After Tower Bridge the marathon route heads towards the City and for about a mile the road is divided in two with runners going in each direction. Those at thirteen miles are heading east and adjacent to them are the runners already at twenty-two miles, heading for the final stretch. It serves as an almost immediate reality check to the rock-star high of crossing the river. Where minutes ago you felt like an iconic athlete, capable of anything, suddenly you are confronted with a sea of runners all nine miles further along the route.

It was exactly as I hit this point that 'halfway' ceased to sound like an achievement and became more of a sentence. I had to do this all over again? I had already been drenched, tearful, injured, ecstatic and hysterical. Doing it a second time was absurd, out of the question, a nonsense. Yet there seemed no alternative but to keep plodding on.

The crowd started to thin out as some runners slowed to a walk, others stopped to chat to loved ones or queue for a roadside toilet, and some dropped out altogether. The thundering mass that had crossed the bridge where the route was at its narrowest now spread across the wide avenues of the City of London. I could still see runners around me but they were becoming fewer and fewer. There was no one close enough to talk to any more, no one's feet to stare at as I tried to convince myself that the end would appear soon. There were barely any spectators. The space I had craved a couple of hours earlier now felt like a cruel echo chamber.

Bereft of the iconic sights that we had passed earlier, feeling increasingly isolated and bombarded by encroaching tiredness, my mind began to play tricks on me. While my legs seemed able to keep going my mental strength was collapsing. I began not just to doubt myself, but to berate myself. *You're running around the City in a pair of ripped trousers to try and prove a point about respect that you could just have discussed with people. You wouldn't be feeling like this if you had trained properly. All those runs where you didn't try your hardest because you were 'a bit tired', well, this is tiredness. You're weak because you're tired, you probably won't make it. You're weak even to be considering the fact that you won't make it. You're selfish, making your friends and family come and cheer for you when you're not even that good. You're not tired, you're just lazy.*

The torrent of self-doubt continued for mile upon mile, added to which the pain in my pelvis was growing. Soulless concrete and glass buildings dominated the landscape, growing ever taller as the route became more intricate between miles fifteen and twenty. The mile markers were out of sight and we were running in loops, weaving between huge office blocks that hid from view the next water station or cheering point. Just as I needed it most my faith utterly vanished like an amaretti wrapper in flames.

I had devoted so much attention and preparation to avoiding hitting The Wall, but I had devoted nothing at all to avoiding this emotional wall. No one had warned me about it, no one had told me how to prevent it, no one had prepared me for how to deal with it. Was I the only one feeling these things? Of course I assumed that I was, as I was most certainly the most pathetic runner of the pack. I would have been prepared to argue until sundown with anyone who had told me that I could do it at this point. Even the most well-meaning roadside cheers were now reaching my ears as jeers. I wanted to hide from them all, to conceal this certain humiliation. I was sure to the point of rage that this race was never going to end. For the first time all day there was no doubt in my mind. This was nothing to do with nutrition, or tiredness, or hormones. Those were ludicrous suggestions. Mental doors suggesting any other possibility slammed shut the second I approached them: it was simple, I would be running for ever.

The last remaining shred of impetus that kept me putting one foot in front of the other was that of the sponsorship money I had raised. As much as the training had been an epic journey, so had the fund-raising. Sense is a charity that does amazing work with families of deaf-blind children. Vanessa, the friend who had pointed me in the direction of that charity, had been part of the team for years. I had seen photographs of events, I had met her colleagues in the pub, I had heard about families she had worked with. I tried to replace the image I had of me weeping by the side of the road with the far more emotive images of these children. I tried to remind myself — out loud at times — that my pain was temporary, whereas their hardships were permanent. I tried to remember the good training days I'd had, to feel strong for the people I was running for, to achieve what they might never be able to. Then I texted my dad.

'Looks like I won't make it. Very weak now'

'Don't be ridiculous. Just tiredness. We are close'

'WHERE probably going to stop soon cant go on'

'BENEATH ONE CANADA SQUARE'

'What? We dont even go there'

'You do can see other runners now'

'Wont see you. Must have passed'

'What mile are you on? You will see us. The crowd is ready for you'

'Wont. Will probably just stop'

'KEEP GOING WE ARE NEAR'

That was it. I had missed them. The idiots were standing in the wrong place. My father had probably been staring at an unnecessary map as I'd passed, while my mother and sister gossiped. I bet they had all seen my brother, who didn't even need any support. Tears streamed down my face, my pelvis creaked with pain every time my right foot hit the road. I resigned myself once again to the hopelessness of my cause as I rounded yet another corner to yet another tedious urban vista. Stupid bloody London.

I stared at my feet, grimly plodding forward. *Keep going, keep going*, I muttered to myself. It began to feel as if everyone around me was doing the same. I looked up. Everyone around me *was* doing the same. And there was my family surrounded by a huge group of forty or fifty total strangers they seem to have rallied to cheer when I appeared. 'Keep going,' they were yelling. 'Keep going!'

My mother's hair was a bird's nest of excitement and weather. 'I can't even believe that there IS a place called Mudchute, let ALONE that I'm in it on a Sunday morning!' Her hands were thrown in the air in confused horror as I spotted them. My sister was in tears and delirious with giggles at my mother. My father was grinning from ear to ear. 'I told you,' he mouthed. I ran to the side of the road and flung myself at him for a hug. I felt my sister gingerly stroking my hair. Everyone around them carried on cheering, telling me I could make it, explaining how long they'd

126

been waiting to see me and how much they had heard about my fall. My father placed his curved hand beneath my chin and lifted it to meet his gaze.

'You will finish this. You have done the hardest part. You are strong.'

I bleated about my sore pelvis, my tiredness, my despair. But he wouldn't have it. He would not countenance the idea that I might not finish. There was no arguing with his calm, granite faith in me. I hugged him again and rejoined the route. My legs remained exhausted but my heart felt lighter. There was hope. I passed Captain Caveman's club, tossed to the side of the road with the discarded water bottles, and hoped he was feeling OK too. We began to weave away from the heart of the City and the crowd seemed to get thicker again as the roads narrowed. I remembered one of the nuggets of advice my father had given us at lunch the previous day: just talk to someone if you get lonely. You don't have to run alone.

I felt a tap on my shoulder and turned round. A young man's face smiled at me and asked me to move aside. I did, confused by what seemed a very formal way to approach the simple step of overtaking someone. I saw two men behind him, strapped to each other with the kind of wrist lead that I had only ever seen on toddlers in supermarkets before. The older of the two men was blind, the younger was leading him. And the third man, who had tapped my shoulder, was clearing a path for them.

For a few hundred metres I watched the team, marvelling at how fit the third man must be to circle his team like that. I truly understood what 'running rings around someone' meant as he danced about, covering twice their distance, alerting other runners to their approach with an effortless charm. It seemed easy to slot in behind them, watching the blind man's feet and using them as a pace guide while taking advantage of the small oasis of calm behind them. After half a mile one of them offered some of the sweets that they were eating. I took a cola bottle and thanked him profusely. The third man smiled and asked how I was getting on. I explained that my mood was clearing now, but that it had been dark for a while.

'It's a big deal, running a marathon,' he reassured me, despite barely having broken a sweat and continuing to run rings around us to create space.

'Is it your first time?' I asked timidly.

'No, this is our seventh.'

'Wow, you've run seven marathons! All together?'

'Yes, we've done them in the last seven days.'

'You've run ... seven marathons in ... seven days?'

'Yes, this is Blind Dave. He's doing it for charity.'

My head was spinning. They had been doing this every day for a week. Yet they seemed like the most sunny-natured people I'd encountered all day. I wanted to hug them all, but was reluctant to break their chirpy stride. So I ran alongside them for four or five miles, sharing food, water and anecdotes about the day. My father had of course been right. Just chatting to people distracted me from the now-excruciating pain in my hips and knees. They kept my mind busy, away from self-destructive ridiculousnesses, and they reminded me how fleeting my own pain was. God knows how their hips and knees felt after seven marathons.

We headed away from the City and along the Embankment to the final stretch. The crowds of spectators suddenly increased in size and the cheering became frenzied. My grin was back. I was going to make it after all. I was looking around as the sites loomed into view. The river, the London Eye, the parks. I didn't care how my feet felt any more. I knew I was going to make it.

'You look like you're perking up,' said my new running pal. 'You should speed up for the last mile, do it in style. But make sure you enjoy it.'

So I did.

From somewhere a final, desperate surge of energy bubbled up and propelled me faster, away from Blind Dave and his helpers. Everything I had felt at the eighteen-mile point flipped into reverse. Every single training run suddenly made sense as my legs found the power to overtake handfuls of people while still grinning and waving at the onlookers. I wasn't a failure, I wasn't pathetic, I wasn't weak. I had proved that I could set myself a goal and meet it. I had shown that I could redefine who I was and who I could be. I had discovered that tenacity in myself as well as a huge well of goodwill in my friends and loved ones.

I was literally following in my father's footsteps. I was being driven by his faith in me, in the texts I'd received all day from him and others. I was doing it for all of them. Riding a tide of adrenalin I felt the strongest I ever had. I was proud of myself and proud that others were proud of me. I saw children catching sight of their loved ones and felt proud of everyone around me. My legs were getting stronger as we approached Big Ben and then curved towards the Mall. I was a tourist attraction, a superhero, a medal winner.

The finish line seemed to be coming towards me as every part of my body heaved with the final effort and an all-consuming relief that I was about to cross the line. As I approached it there was only one thought in my mind: I am never, ever doing that again. My feet carried me over the line and I threw my hands above my head to look up at the red banner. That thought was immediately replaced by another: Next time I think I could probably do it a bit faster.

7

The London Marathon. Again

'In running it doesn't matter if you come in first, in the middle of the pack, or last. You can say 'I have finished.' There is a lot of satisfaction in that.'
>   Fred Lebow, New York City
>   marathon co-founder

I glided through that summer after my first marathon basking in the shimmery golden rays of my victory. At meetings, at weddings, at Sunday lunches, people who hadn't seen me for a while wanted to catch up on every detail of the impossible feat I had performed. How on earth had I managed it? How had I trained? How had I discovered I could do such a thing? I was the Girl Who Did, an inspiration to all!

Convinced I would be a runner for life I was high on my achievement and thrilled by others' fascination with it. I glowed when strangers would hear me chatting to my friends about it and sought my advice. I would give it freely. People nodded thoughtfully as I blessed

132

them with my knowledge, while I was intrigued by how obvious it usually was: the only answer I ever had for those who said they would never be able to make it further than 5 km was that 'You have to decide to. You just have to want to.' Because that was all I had done. I had wanted to.

But somewhere in my subconscious something was shifting. A tense was changing. An opaqueness was settling over my marathon glow. I started to refer to my running self as an other self, a temporary self, a self who had been built to make an impact not to withstand one. I heard myself referring to what I had done rather than what I did. A subtle resignation to that experience being an exceptional time in my life seemed to settle in. I was not a runner — I had run.

The physical act of running slowly returned to being something hypothetical: something that celebrities did to sell DVDs, something that shallow people tormented themselves with in order to stay slim, something that others did with elan while I pottered along with my handbag and a Crunchie. As for the psychological side it must have been something I'd made up. It felt like a fad, like the time that I decided to study homeopathy, or the year I spent convinced that Simon Cowell was sexy.

I had never imagined that it would all go away again just as fast as I had created it, if not faster. I was exhausted and the thought of running was repulsive to me. The sports kit I had chosen so carefully now seemed as alien to me as school uniform. Once so familiar it was now merely representative of a stage in my life, now over. I had thought I'd become a runner. I had just become someone who could run a marathon. I didn't know how different the two were back then.

Within a year of finishing that first London Marathon I was no longer running. Perhaps I was making it round the park once a month, but I was getting progressively less fit, less healthy and less happy. I had done a marathon, so why did I need to run any more? The motivation had deserted me. My toenails grew back and with them a layer of extra me. My muscles softened, my heart slowed and my skin grew dull again. I focused on other things — I changed the way I worked, I moved from London to Brighton and I made new friends.

That first summer living in Brighton I was exhausted, unhealthy and heartbroken. I had started smoking again and felt ashamed when I saw London friends who still associated me with a swooshing ponytail and a pair of trainers. But there was one remaining thread of healthiness that kept me going: the seafront. As I had done three years previously I walked myself happy. I left my flat, still mesmerised by the fact that I lived with the sea on my doorstep, and headed either east or west along the coast. I walked everywhere, down the hill to the seafront, along the beach to wherever I needed to be and then back up. I don't drive, there was no Tube and I didn't understand the strange buses in my new city or know where the names on their stops were. While I could see the South Downs as I whizzed through them on the way back from a party or a meeting in London, the rest of my new home went largely unexplored.

Then, with a lightning bolt, everything changed. A friend needed me. My pal Julia, who had been so utterly steadfast in her support over my horrible summer, asked me to run the London Marathon with her. One of her dearest friends had died suddenly from a particularly aggressive form of cancer. He had gone from diagnosis to death in a matter of weeks and left Julia and their social circle poleaxed by shock and grief. Julia, who had a toddler at home and was utterly devastated by how the summer had ended, was overwhelmed by the need to do something with her pain. She had to pay tribute, create some good from the suffering, do something that would make her friend proud.

Julia is not a woman who makes false promises, or one to ask favours easily. One of my most inspiring 'can do' friends, she had long been the one I would turn to for some undiluted real talk when things were hard. She had long been the first to tell me when a boyfriend was 'good for nothing beyond giving you wet shoulders', her expression for men who just ended up weeping on me. She never hesitated to encourage me when I pondered over a job opportunity I wasn't sure I had the skills for. She was strong. So to see her weakened was not just upsetting, but profoundly unusual. It convinced me more than ever that anything really is possible. If she were to pull through something that could make her seem so frail she would need every scrap of help I could give her.

I had by now spent the last couple of years comfortably saying I would never run the London Marathon again: I would never get a place, I would never find the time to train and I would never be as young again. These weren't excuses; they were things I genuinely believed to be true. If there was no need, why should I do it? Now there was need.

'It doesn't matter if we walk it,' she said, 'I just need someone to be there with me, someone who knows what it's all like.'

When someone you love has a loved one taken away when they least expect it you cannot say no to anything that might ease their grief. Committing to help Julia run in memory of her dear friend Jerome was a decision I didn't hesitate over. Seeing her visible pain created a rush of 'What's the worst that could happen? My toes might hurt but that's it.' It hadn't been that bad, had it?

Before I knew it I was going to run my second marathon, and on top of that I was helping another person through it. Now I had to convince someone else that they could run, that they would finish, that it would be worth it, not just myself.

We committed to raising a large amount of money for the Institute of Cancer Research. As we started training — Julia in London, me in Brighton, our online communication constant, — I came to realise that having done one marathon a huge part of the fear I once had was gone from my running self. For one simple reason: I knew what to expect. I knew what the emotional dips were and where they were likely to come. I knew what it felt like to need the loo on a long run and to overcome it (or not). And I knew with absolute certainty that I could finish a marathon.

I also remembered that I had grown up in

an environment where feats of endurance were if not expected then accepted. My father's marathon prowess meant that he'd had zero hesitation when he told me I could run that first marathon. And my mother's side of the family are all from Trinidad — veterans of carnival. And what is carnival if not a marathon — two days spent on your feet wearing bright skimpy clothes, sweating profusely as you tread and retread the streets of the capital while people hand you sugary drinks. I'd had one of the greatest tools that a first-time marathoner can get their hands on: people around me with absolute faith that I would complete, even if I did not yet believe it myself. And that was a tool I was determined to equip Julia with. Bigger than me and even less sporty than I had been when I began running, she was going to need it.

The training started well. My campaign of confidence brainwashing was working and Julia made incredible (not literal) leaps. In a matter of weeks she transformed herself from a woman who thought that the idea of her getting round the park was hilarious, to one who could confidently complete five kilometres half walking, half jogging. And then one who could run the whole way. Best of all she seemed to be enjoying it. Having spent the last year or so at home looking after her little boy she visibly relished the little pockets of space in her day that running created. She could clear her head, and lose herself in the endorphins fired off by her pumping legs. She realised that running with a hangover was not the worst thing on earth and it often got rid of that hangover altogether. Her confidence, so shaken by grief, started to return. She literally started to get a glow in her cheeks. Julia was back.

Meanwhile in Brighton I was reaquainting myself with the very idea of running, let alone running itself. I had agreed to take part in this epic mission without hesitation and with little or no consideration of what it was going to mean for me. My only reservation was not that I might not finish it, but that the relentlessness and commitment of training would bore me all over again. Where once I had got to know London's parks, hills and backstreets, my beloved Brighton seafront now seemed rather limiting. One of the greatest joys of my previous marathon training had been the huge variety of landscapes I'd encountered: cemeteries, wiggling seventeenth-century streets, wide sloping Regency terraces, the wilds of Hampstead Heath. Now my runs would have the same two views for the next six months. You go one way and you see the Palace Pier or the Marina. You go the other and you see the West Pier and Shoreham power station.

Except that wasn't what happened at all. The view was never the same, not once. As I began to train I started to notice the subtle movement of the tide — something that I had never spotted while walking, phone in hand, checking messages and chatting to mates. I saw how the birds circled at different times of day depending on how much food had been left on the beach by the tourists. I watched the shape and colour of the sea change and mottle according to the weather and the contents of the sky above.

As autumn slowly turned to winter and the clocks changed, I learned what the seafront looked like at dusk and then in the dark. I started to cherish the sight of the sea at night and with it the magical feeling of having my eyes open but seeing only darkness, as if I could just run off the edge of the world. I began to recognise the chandeliers and the fanciest paintings on the walls of the largest homes in the smartest crescents on the seafront. And I was soon able to identify the party flats in the blocks rising above it, smiling to myself at the coloured lights flashing within. I watched surfers dancing on the surface of the sea at dusk and ran for four miles watching a murmuration of starlings.

I learned about the Undercliff Walk, a wide esplanade cut into the chalky cliffs, running from Brighton Marina to Saltdean in the east. I would run along it, basking in the glare of the winter sun, then turn and make my way back along the top of the cliffs, feeling once again as if I really were only a few steps from flying. I would watch the Palace Pier twinkling at dusk as the lights came on and see the West Pier seeming to bob up and down with my own movement, like a regal spider in the bath.

On New Year's Day I ran for a mile behind two shivering Goths, one of whom seemed to hover like a Dalek in a bin bag. They hugged and huddled against each other and as I finally caught up with and then passed them I wanted to hug them both. As January took flight I watched teams of workmen repaint the pale green Victorian railings along the front, taking a few each day, slowly making progress. Each morning I would say hello and congratulate them on getting a little further.

As I needed to add extra miles to my runs I would wiggle down little streets lined with fishermen's cottages that I had never come across before. I discovered hidden alleyways that seemed to have been created in the imagination of Daphne du Maurier or at the very least Captain Jack Sparrow. I found parks I never knew the city had, I discovered little Tudor-style cottages and pockets of mid-century design away from the endless wedding-cake prettiness of the creamy Regency seafront.

I felt myself become part of my new city, as it became part of me. I ran along the pier early one February morning, raising my head to expose my throat to a seagull hovering above me, searching for doughnuts to grab. Then I dropped my gaze to see the sea raging beneath the wooden slats of the pier. Sandwiched between gull and pier I had never felt happier, or more like I belonged somewhere. I started to understand the weird mists that could appear over the sea but never seem to make it to land. And in turn I myself became part of the view. A runner whizzing past the tourists who dawdled past the shops of flip-flops and ornaments made from shells. Just as I enjoyed the landscape of my new city I was also absorbed into it. Like the laces pulling the two sides of my trainers together, running was meshing me and my home ever closer together.

It didn't feel as if I was falling back in love with running, it felt as if I was falling deeply in love with Brighton. For the first time in my life I had chosen a city and become a part of it, let it truly become part of my identity. My hair was now salty with sea spray wherever I was. And all this time my legs were still moving beneath me. I was barely noticing them, so caught up in my new relationship was I. What could have been boredom became a meditation, a way of learning more about my city. Not having yet reached a point where my runs were pushing me I was able to enjoy them, thinking about the end goal and basking in the process and my surroundings.

But just as I was enjoying the gifts of running more than ever, Julia was starting to struggle with the enormity of what she had taken on. Sadness continued to wave over her and with it the brutal confusion of grieving for someone who had died far too young. As the training for the marathon made its gentle transition from learning to run to knuckling down to build long-term endurance, I noticed a slight shift in her attitude towards herself. She was starting to prepare the ground not for victory, but for potential failure. She suffered an injury that caused her a huge amount of pain. She became scared to run because of the pain it caused, yet running less meant that when she braved a run it hurt more. Her confidence stalled, then started to ebb away. She worried about not spending enough time with her son, she worried about the amount of money we were committed to raising, she worried about the idea of letting anyone down.

Watching her I remembered the cast-iron belief I'd once had that I could never ever run a marathon. I remembered my father's calm, consistent confidence in me and how at times a particularly bad run felt like a sort of defiance against him. That crystal-clear recollection was not of doubting that I might not make it, but of knowing it. But now I knew I could, and I knew she could . . . but I didn't know how to convince her.

'But you're so much fitter than me,' Julia would say.

'Only because I did the training,' I would reply.

'But you're a natural runner,' she would say.

'No I am not! Have you seen my boobs? I was not born a runner; I became one.'

I tried everything I could think of to reignite her self-belief — joking, pushing, ignoring, cajoling, recruiting mutual friends, but there was no convincing her. She firmly believed it was not possible.

One time, during a fund-raising quiz night that we'd put on I heard her husband reassuring Julia that it didn't matter if she didn't make it. I felt not warmth but despair. How dare he undermine her like this? How

144

dare he undermine my hard work like this? It felt like he was deliberately fuelling her self-doubt. I was furious. (It was only years later when someone said the same to me that I understood how what had seemed like a total lack of faith on his part was actually the kindest sort of unconditional love.)

As marathon day approached Julia and I became locked in what was now a strange benign battle of wills: she became ever more convinced that she couldn't do it, and I remained sure that she could. It was as if we were determined to prove each other wrong. She was painfully embarrassed to try and even run in front of me, despite being strong and significantly leaner than ever before.

At one point the only thing that seemed to be pushing both of us forward was the fact that we were managing to raise significantly more money than we had dared to hope. We asked everyone we knew for help, and everyone that they knew. It was crucial that this whole endeavour had some sort of tangible result and we both started compulsively checking our JustGiving site to see how the donations were totting up.

We auctioned film and TV memorabilia that we'd managed to beg, steal and borrow. Julia arranged a sell-out night of live comedy as well as the aforementioned quiz night. I wrote about our project in *Red* magazine and we both charted our progress online wherever we could. Entire families were involved, whole friendship groups. A community grew. I hoped that Julia felt the swell of goodwill towards us when she doubted herself in the dead of night, because it was certainly there and at times it was all that kept me going as I tried to keep spirits and confidence high. Our charity was thrilled and gave us two tickets for supporters to sit with the press and VIPs at the finish line. Julia decided that she wanted her husband and friends along the course, so they were sent to my delighted father.

Meanwhile, as training progressed, the weather forecasts flip-flopped insanely between the temperatures of mid-winter and mid-summer. On one of my final training runs, a seventeen-mile slog, while Julia was getting drenched running along the South Bank it was so hot in Brighton that I ran into the sea. It was the closest I have ever come to heatstroke — the white chalk of the cliffs glowing under the beam of the sun. I dreamt of water, imagined it oozing from the ground. My tongue seemed to be growing inside of my mouth, like that of a dog stuck in a hot car. I remembered from old Enid Blyton books that I shouldn't drink from the sea. Instead I waded in, ankle deep. I looked around. There were women in bikinis on the beach. It was March. I took off my running top and dipped it in the icy water. I wrung it out and put it back on. The fabric stuck to my skin, cooling me down with reassuring speed. I would make it, we would make it.

Slowly, slowly, slowly we became fitter. The weekend before the race was a dear friend's hen party in Dorset, which I attended without touching a drop of alcohol and still had the time of my life. My confidence in my body had returned, as had my enjoyment of food and its disassociation from guilt and shame. Once more I was proud to be able to *do* rather than to watch. I had spent the entire afternoon's coasteering leaping happily from rocks into the sea like a chirpy little mountain goat. Julia texted me a couple of times, terrified that I would hurt myself and be unable to run. What she didn't know is that even if the rocks of Dorset's Jurassic coastline had smashed both of my legs to smithereens she would still not have tackled that marathon alone. I was ready.

It was not until a few days later when we went to the London Marathon Expo in Docklands that Julia finally allowed herself to believe that she might make the finish line. Held at the enormous and terrifying Excel conference centre the Expo is a three-day event where competitors collect their running numbers, their running chips and final information regarding the event. They are then bombarded by countless stands and stalls pitching future events all over the world, as well as every conceivable type of running kit, shoe, food and accessory. The day of the Expo visit is simultaneously hugely reassuring and leg-numbingly scary. On the one hand you are confronted with a world of running that has previously been rather limited to running magazines, TV footage or word of mouth. It is like Mecca, making you feel tiny, insignificant and overwhelmed by the numbers involved. On the other hand it comforts you with the fact that the vast majority of the other runners are normal people, people just like you. They are dads with their kids, grannies with their family, friends supporting friends and large charity groups egging each other on. And among them there are many who, like Julia, are undertaking the challenge not for bravado-instilling bucket-list reasons, but for emotional ones. They are making a tribute, they are offering up their suffering to help others who have suffered worse.

On entering the hall there was a large white wall steadily becoming filled with scribbled-on messages and dedications. Julia wrote a small note to Jerome and I signed a note next to it in support of her. As we stepped back and looked at our tiny handwriting, almost lost in the sea of others' jottings, our hearts were in our throats. I put my hand out and held hers. We were going to do this. We were part of something bigger than us now. And we would see it through to the end.

But first we had the rest of the Expo to explore, which we did with renewed enthusiasm and lunacy. There are some items of pocket-laden high-tech running kit that merit little attention beyond pointing, laughing and moving on. We even found a Miami-retiree-style sun visor which we tried on merely for the pleasure of a ludicrous photograph. And then there are the people who take it so seriously in their fully kitted-out self-importance that they deserve little more than the befuddled stares we gave them. As the endless marathon theme music (actually the theme music for a 1966 film, *The Trap*, composed by Ron Goodwin, who also composed the score for *Those Magnificent Men in Their Flying Machines* and cult thriller *Village of the Damned*) played on a loop throughout the hall I felt the excitement of the day start to infuse Julia with a little more optimism than she'd had for months. Surrounded by the crowds, the music and the garish running outfits we found a couple of small chinks of quiet, and grinned at each other. We're going to be OK. It's worth it. So it's going to be OK.

On the morning of the event itself I woke up as sick with nerves as I had done three years ago. But this time the nerves were not about whether I could get myself round the course (which was suddenly feeling like less of a certainty) but more about whether I could get Julia round it. She was still incredibly nervous and while her anxieties had ebbed a little — and her sense of humour was doing its best to mask them — the importance of her finishing had seemed to grow with each passing day. For Jerome, for those who had helped us with the fund-raising, for those at the Royal Marsden Hospital who would be helped by the money, and for our apparently eternally patient loved ones. We had to do them all proud.

We met at Blackheath station, where Julia presented me with a huge HEMMO badge to sew onto the front of my running top. As with the start of all public races there was little space or equipment for dignity, so I whipped out the needle and thread I'd brought along and started to stitch. Once in Greenwich Park we checked our bags in at the luggage trucks, and I watched the dismay flicker across Julia's face as she realised like I had that she had just surrendered her valuables to a total stranger.

We took our positions in the penultimate pen and waited for the start of the race to be announced. All around us the hubbub of runners, costumes, supporters and the incessant PA system playing 'inspiring' eighties music created a kind of mental carnival for those of us feeling fraught, until eventually we surrendered and joined in with the whooping and clapping ourselves. The countdown to the start was shouted out by all of us and then the crowd burst into cheers. We were off. Once again it took a good five or ten minutes to cross the starting line, going at barely more than a shuffle, but as we did Julia shrieked, 'We're running the bloody London Marathon!'

'We so are! We so bloody are!' I shrieked back.

As before and as with all big races there are a few minutes — maybe even half an hour — where you run along, almost in a trance, semi-hypnotised by the unfamiliar sound of hundreds of other runners around you. The thud thud of trainers, the whispers of breath, the feeling that you can't stop because you're moving as a pack now and no one's getting left behind. I tried not to talk for a bit, hoping that Julia would absorb and enjoy this moment, letting confidence and pride seep in.

We ran in silence for a while before I cracked and let out the first of many hollers on seeing our friends Jon and Dave standing at the side of the road. Arms crossed, feet hip-width apart and eyes glazed, they had the steely stare of a pair of builders working out a quote for a particularly nasty job but was actually a result of hunting us out from a sea of people. They had led the charge with teasing us about training over the last few months and now they were there for us. Up early on a Sunday, as steadfast and honourable as I'd always suspected they were.

'GUYS!' I shouted and their blank gazes broke into goofy grins and big lollopy waves. They shouted back and carried on cheering us until we were long gone. I felt a lump in my throat that the first of many supporters had seen us making a go of it. And Julia was glowing at the sheer exhilaration of being cheered in the streets.

The bands, the crowds, the children with their little pots of jelly beans: the atmosphere alone kept us going for the first few miles. Soon we were approaching Tower Bridge and the halfway mark. The heat was rising. It was a relentlessly sunny day. As with the weeks before the event the weather had been wildly unpredictable, before finally settling on 'blazing summer's day'. There wasn't a cloud in the sky and the air was warm rather than crisp and fresh. Trying on those sun visors suddenly didn't seem as ridiculous as it had at the time, given that we were now both wearing caps. I kept encouraging Julia to drink water and was barely without a bottle in my hand myself. It seemed prudent to walk for a portion of each mile, rather than to overheat before the end. Even the spectators looked roasting.

But as we got to the bridge I told Julia we should run. 'You don't want to wake up tomorrow and say that you walked over Tower Bridge,' I insisted.

'I'm not sure, I'm not sure how well I'm doing,' she replied.

'It doesn't matter! We're not going for a time! It's an experience you'll never repeat!'

'I don't know . . . '

'Please! For me! Why don't you run ahead a bit and I'll take a picture!'

Julia was persuaded. The photograph I took is one of my favourites, with her looking over one shoulder and an image of Jerome on the back of her T-shirt. We held hands aloft over the second half of the bridge, screaming with delight.

But not long after the halfway mark the heat and the exhaustion started to take its toll. The sunshine was merciless; there didn't seem to be enough water on earth to keep us cool. I tried pouring it down the back of Julia's neck and we both took it in turns to run, squealing, through the showers at the side of the road.

When you're running, heat doesn't just make you feel hot — it chips away at your reality, slowly but surely. It makes your feet feel as if you're wearing someone else's oversized shoes. It makes your tongue feel as if you have just woken up with the worst hangover of your life. And worst of all it can confuse you. Distances start to lose perspective, limbs feel heavy and words begin to jumble.

What are perfectly normal, reasonable physiological responses to heat suddenly feel like emotional Armageddon. While I knew that the third quarter of a marathon felt like hell I knew that it didn't last for ever, but Julia did not. And to watch her slump was heart-rending. The longer a run is the less it becomes about running. I do not mean that you don't have to keep putting one leg in front of the other, or that you get a free pass on making your heart and lungs work harder. These things all still have to happen. What I mean is that they become the easy bits. The real challenge is dealing with the emotion of it, keeping the mind from collapsing. And as anyone who has started from scratch knows, utterly sure that they won't make it to the end of the road, emotions carried around for several miles can feel heavier than hell itself.

As our pace slowed and our faces reddened I watched, feeling utterly helpless, as Julia started to lose every last scrap of self-belief. To say that she was now convinced we wouldn't finish would be an understatement — she seemed almost affronted that I still had the temerity to suggest otherwise. Ever grateful that I had been down this dark road before and slugged it out with my dad, I let her protestations ride over me and just kept talking, kept encouraging, kept distracting. At times I was so hot that I wasn't sure if I was hallucinating myself. Words upon words came spilling out of my mouth, until I no longer really knew what my latest profundity was. A quote from Eleanor Roosevelt? Or perhaps just something from *Dawson's Creek*? No matter, as long as we kept going forward, forward.

As we passed more friends our spirits were raised once more, their grins and tears convincing us it was worth it after all. There were a few miles where I felt Julia was truly at her darkest, almost physically exfoliating herself of layer upon layer of grief. Her emotional pain was now being mirrored by considerable physical pain and it was this that she focused on. If she could cry here on the street maybe there would be less sadness when she got home, I reasoned.

Slowly, eventually, we turned onto the Embankment and there we saw more faces of those we knew and loved. I had been promising her the high of this last mile for hours now. For months I had been telling her that this moment would be worth it. And then we were there. But even as we turned onto the Mall she was expressing doubt that she would make it.

'I can carry you from here!' I yelled, sure that her spirits would rally soon.

'Oh my god, oh my god.'

'What?'

'I can see the finish line!' A huge grin cracked her face. Finally she knew she could do it.

As we ran towards the finish line I took her hand. Suddenly we heard people shouting our names. I couldn't work out where it was coming from. Then, suddenly, as we approached the gallery of press seats at the finish line I saw my parents. My father in his seat, grinning and waving wildly. And my mother, who was shrieking and clambering down from the seats and onto the side of the track. Her tiny legs scuttled towards us as the sound of her voice cut over the music and cheering.

'GO GO GO ALEX AND JULIA YOU ARE THE BEST YOU MUST KEEP GOING EVERYONE IS SO PROUD OF YOU YOU HAVE NO IDEA HOW PROUD WE ALL ARE AND NOW IT IS THE FINISH JUST ENJOY IT I HAVE BEEN SITTING HERE ALL DAY AND SEEN SO MUCH BORING SPORT AND NOW YOU ARE FINALLY HERE OH THANK GOD GO GOGOGO ALEX AND JULIA . . . '

She was off the seating area now and running alongside us, my father behind her in the stands, taking photographs. And she continued to run along with us, screaming, until we ran our final steps. We crossed the finish line, grinning, crying, holding hands.

We had done it.

We were given our medals, collected our bags and headed to the crowd of friends and family waiting for us with hugs, food and congratulations. A friend's little boy paraded around wearing my medal, convinced he had won the marathon himself. My mother cried and stroked my hair. Julia hugged her son, who was wearing her medal.

We had done it.

★　★　★

I lay face down on a massage table the next day, staring at the masseuse's feet — a moment of stillness after the shouting, heaving, weeping of the previous day. I watched the feet shuffle gently out of view and realised that something had shifted in me that spring. While you, and only you, can move your legs from start to finish no one runs a marathon alone. I had supported Julia, but I had received great support myself. My friends and family knew how hard I'd found it and they had been wonderful. But what I had really learned was that running could no longer be about me and my personal goals any more. To go that far, to feel that pain, to endure that depth of despair, it had to be about more than my own self-worth, it had to have a purpose beyond me. I couldn't just continue running around in circles. As soon as I could I opened my laptop and bought places for several races over the course of the next year: the Royal Parks Half Marathon, the White Night Half Marathon, the Brighton Half Marathon and the Brighton Marathon. I had to reach further. I had to reach beyond myself.

8

A Runner for Life?

*'Methinks that the moment my legs begin
to move, my thoughts begin to flow . . . '*
Henry David Thoreau

My ambition in those first few days after my
second London Marathon was at an all-time
high. Without Julia to coax I was sure that
finally I would touch the very outer limits of
my ability. I had given myself two months to
rest before training again for two half marathons which were to take place in October,
another in February, followed by the Brighton
Marathon the next April. These would be my
real runs, my masterworks. I would discover
the truth about myself on those courses and
then head to Edinburgh to conquer Arthur's
Seat. An enlightenment awaited me, for sure.

A week later I was on holiday in Rome,
hobbling around the Forum on still-tired feet
and burying my face in pasta at every available
opportunity. A month later I was still working
on my training plans with all the earnest
indolence of a student making multicoloured

revision cards. Six months later, after some fitful training, I was wondering what had become of my enlightenment.

★ ★ ★

It was 1 a.m. My mind was as awash with regret as my legs were with mud. I put my foot forward, hoping that this time it would hit hard ground as I landed. Nope. Another puddle. This one was deeper than the last. I felt cold mud splatter up the back of my thigh through my running tights as I kicked my heel up and plundered forward. I adjusted my head torch and tried to see where the next mile marker might be. As I turned my head it caught two flashing lights: not cat's eyes on the road, but a pair of cow's eyes, staring at me from a few metres away. Was that mud I had been splashing through or cow pats? I ran on.

I was making my way through a field on the South Downs, receiving evil looks from sleepy cows. The last month had been a bit much — my brother-in-law's illness, the birth of my nephew and the considerable indignity of the Royal Parks Half Marathon. Nevertheless I was running again. This time it was the White Night Half Marathon, taking place on the night the clocks went back. Starting from the seafront at midnight my brother and I were taking part in a run that then took us up and out of Brighton and across the Downs before heading back down into Hove. I was exhausted, and worst of all I was full.

'Let's make a weekend of it!' I had told my brother cheerfully, six months before. 'I'll make lasagne and then we can go for a massive roast the next day!'

He had not taken long to persuade and after what had felt like far too little time training we soon found ourselves eating that lasagne, our running kit laid out ready for the late-night race. I had never run at night before. What was more confusing — troubling even — was not the darkness itself but the confusion over when to eat. Everything I had learned before had involved a good meal of carbohydrates the night before and then a relatively normal breakfast the next morning. But a night run? When do you eat? How do you get the carbs in? At lunchtime? And are you supposed to have breakfast in the evening? What if you get hungry? Or if you're too full?

We settled on an early supper at 6 p.m. Seven hours later we regretted it. Within half an hour of setting off I was still able to feel the supper jiggling around inside of me. Both plates of it. For the first mile or two, running through the city centre being cheered on by stags and hens and partygoers, I had

161

managed to stay distracted. But now William was way ahead of me. He had made an early departure from the middle of the pack, with a group of earnest-looking men in expensive-looking kit. I had managed to leave those in actual fancy dress behind me and was feeling increasingly lonely among a handful of distinctly average runners. And now I was running through country roads on the outskirts of Brighton, starting to panic about how much I needed the loo.

It was a small race and most runners were either hardcore sporty types who were in it for the experience or fun runners from the British Heart Foundation, who were the main sponsor. I seemed to be the only runner who was neither. Street after street went by of suburban bungalows with immaculate front lawns, dotted with tiny grinning gnomes. My feet went onwards, onwards as only one thought made an everlasting circuit around my mind: Is it better to be woken at home by a sweaty runner begging to use your bathroom, or to find one squatting on your front lawn with her jogging bottoms around her ankles?

Neither seemed preferable. Both were possible.

The residential roads continued on a slight incline until we were running above Brighton, looking down on its twinkling lights and beyond it the blackness of the sea. I put my hand to my stomach. I felt the elastic of my running tights straining against it. Why lasagne, why? Once my true love, now my sworn enemy. I felt another bubbly rumble. I ran on, my top lip sweating despite the cold.

Then in the distance I saw the lights. Like Mary and Joseph before me I came upon an inn! It was not strictly an inn, but a local pub with a Thai night on Saturdays. The lights were still on, they must still be open! I looked at my watch: it was just before 1 a.m. It seemed very unlikely that a pub in such a quiet area would still be open, but the lights . . . the lights. I almost sprinted to the door and hammered on it, crying, 'Is anyone in there?'

A smiling man answered the door. 'Hello, love.'

'Hi, hi, I'm so sorry, are you still open?'

'No, love, that's why the door's locked.'

'Oh no, may I use your bathroom?'

'We've just cleaned it.' He eyed me up and down, his face indicating that he did not trust me to leave his facilities in the condition in which I would find them. I can't swear that there were tears in my eyes at this point, but there must have been a general air of desperation about me as I sighed.

'But go on, love, you look like you need it.' He smiled a smile filled with pity.

'I need it so much,' I replied. 'So, so much.' And I really did.

I left the pub lighter and happier, with a renewed sense of enthusiasm for the run. I bounced past the rest of the residential streets, which eventually gave way to the fields. As we left the suburbs the route took us across the Downs and suddenly the reason we had been given head torches made itself clear. I trampled through field after field, my bearings entirely lost and my perspective starting to fade. It was the first event I had taken part in with absolutely no supporters, and frankly that surly cow was poor compensation.

I took to standing aside a minute to send a desperate email to a group of disparate friends, just to try and pierce the loneliness that was starting to gnaw at me. They were a gang I was in touch with a lot, who had been the first to console me when I had finished the Royal Parks Half Marathon in such a state. It was so late I doubted anyone would reply, but to my surprise I was met with a handful of chatty little messages. One or two of them were in bed watching TV, one was queueing for a club in East London and starting to feel the cold, and another was in a cab on the way home. Each sent a chirpy opener and within five minutes the tone had changed to gentle ribbing. Soon they were just mercilessly teasing me and I giggled as I saw their comments ping onto my phone in the darkness, my heart swelling with gratitude that they understood what I was up to and it was, to them, as normal a Saturday night for me as theirs was for them. But inevitably they logged off. Beckoned to the club, their home or sleep. I was alone again.

I had known despair on long runs before and I had known loneliness in training, but the combination of the isolated route, the darkness and it being way past my bedtime added a sort of fuzzy confusion. Was this a race that was ever going to actually end? I doubted it. Even when we descended back towards Hove, entering the final stretch, I was almost hallucinating. I hit the seafront again and could see the pier once more. Finally home! Except of course if it's 2 a.m. and pitch dark you can see the pier for miles. I wasn't nearly home at all; I still had 15 per cent of the race to go. The pier seemed to shimmer ahead of me, sometimes so close I could touch it, sometimes so far I wasn't even convinced it was more than just a street light reflecting on the water. I plodded on. My brother — who had now finished — texted me to say that I was nearly there. And eventually I was. The first race I had done in my home town and the first to have really left me a physical husk. We headed back to my flat and stayed up chatting for over an hour, the runner's euphoria hitting us too late to be of use and too early to make me think that my next race would be any better. I was shaken. Perhaps my exciting year of running events was a folly, an indulgence. I just didn't seem to be able to keep my head together when it mattered.

But as I had learned at the Royal Parks and as I remembered once the exhaustion of the White Night faded, sometimes the only thing for it is to just keep going and hope that the emotions will pass. You're not going mad; you are merely very tired. I had to keep reminding myself that the intensity of those dark hours were not permanent, whereas the regular bursts of joy that running gave me had a permanence, a rooted sense of me at my very best. I knew I would have to continue.

Slowly, as the seasons changed, so did my legs and my lungs. I ran over the Christmas break and even went for a New Year's Day run after a particularly gleeful New Year's Eve party at a friend's house on the seafront. Queasy from both champagne and dodgy cocktails I left the house on legs like Bambi's, frail but determined to start the year undefeated. I tottered along the seafront, only to be greeted by the entire house party from the night before cheering and whooping from the doorstep as I passed. Walkers, only their eyes visible amidst hats and scarves, turned to stare, curious as to what this lunatic woman shrieking, 'I might yet spew!' at a Regency villa was up to. By the time I was home my hangover was gone, replaced with a more honest tiredness and a renewed sense of my own resilience.

Sixteen weeks later was my birthday, the weekend of the Brighton Half Marathon. Having applied two years earlier and not made it due to food poisoning, then having attempted it the year before with Julia during our London Marathon training and pulled out within a mile on account of further illness, I was worried that I was blighted by my guts when it came to running in my home town. But this year I was the fittest I had ever been. I knew a half marathon was not an unreasonable race and had friends and family, including my now adorably rotund nephew Louis, coming down to cheer me on and enjoy a big birthday lunch afterwards. I wanted it to be a happy race. I decided it would be a happy race.

And perhaps because of that it was. It was the happiest race I have ever run. The moods caused by running are part of such a delicate and mysterious alchemy. I will never forget the boiling rage I experienced on my way through Hyde Park a few years ago. It was a bitterly cold January day, a training run for my first London Marathon. I was aiming for eleven miles, the furthest I had ever run in my life and certainly further than I could possibly have imagined I'd be able to go only three months previously.

The sky was so crisp that the world looked like it was being broadcast in high definition, and the ground underfoot was still frosty in places. I had my hands balled into fists within my running gloves and my phone in the pocket of my thermal running tights. I had managed about five or six miles — which was by then an average mid-week run — without too much of a problem. But only about twenty minutes later I started to feel tragically tired. My fingers were starting to lose sensation in the cold, my face was becoming brittle from bracing itself against the wind and my thighs were starting to feel like liquid lead. I was eight miles in and suddenly sure I would have to lie on Park Lane and beg a taxi to take me home.

And then I saw them. On the north side of the park. Together. The couple holding hands. Nothing wrong with holding hands on a lovely Sunday walk, I can hear you say. But they weren't on a lovely Sunday walk. They were runners. Runners holding hands. A his 'n' hers run. Matching slinky running tights, matching headbands and fully synchronised strides. And then their hands clasped between them. Who does that? And why? Who are these people that are so inseparable that they need physical contact maintained *while* running? My rage was as pure and brilliant as the snow still sitting on the duck pond.

And then there have been the times I have have been frustrated beyond comprehension by dawdling shoppers crossing a road, or desperate with loneliness at the furthest point from home, or almost delirious with joy on realising that I have run for three miles with almost no recollection of doing it at all. And it is these moments of meditative blankness, followed by piercing clarity, that is the feeling you're chasing on the best runs.

For this half marathon I held that feeling, as solid and sparkling as a diamond, for almost the entire run. The weather, the sky and sea were exquisite. I felt as if every breath I took in were going directly to my muscles, my organs, my spirit. I have never felt more like a runner. I don't know why it was. Perhaps it was because instead of running filled with fear I simply wanted to run as quickly as possible, so I could see my friends and family. I was so happy that they had come down to support me on home turf, and so excited to see my new nephew, little Louis. I honestly believed I was running directly into all of their arms that day. I felt golden, untouchable.

After plumbing the emotional depths that I had in the autumn I felt that my suspicions had finally been proved right — you just had to keep at it. You had to decide that it would get better, just as I'd had to decide that I could become a runner. In both instances the training had been entirely secondary to the results of the mental resilience required. Now, as I sat at that table with my most beloved around me, I was reaping the rewards. I hadn't just trained my legs, I was learning to train my brain. They were finally working together instead of against each other. How could I make this last?

Six weeks later I was on another training run, this time a ten-mile race around Salisbury, near to my parents' house. We started at a local sports centre in the city centre and headed up through breathtaking scenery along the Wye Valley. As we chased the river alongside fields full of frolicking springtime lambs and trees groaning with playful birds, I felt a rush at the extraordinary views my running afforded me. As I ran I realised I was going at almost exactly the same pace as two men ahead of me. They looked strong and fit. They had the physique of runners that usually left me far behind within the first half-mile of an event.

One of the greatest joys of running is how unexpected body shapes manage to run at speeds and distances that seem to bear no relation to their size. I have been overtaken by several women at least twenty years older than me on the Brighton seafront (including one, my nemesis, who seems to manage to do it once a month). Similarly, I have overtaken gobsmackingly athletic-looking women who are clearly younger than me but just haven't put in the number of miles that I have. But best of all is overtaking the men. The first time I did this was on one of my first Brighton runs, when I plodded along for about a mile behind a man whose T-shirt declared him 'Born to run' and whose smell betrayed him as a fan of using half a bottle of Lynx instead of a shower.

I tried for about eight minutes to overtake him, knowing that if I were going to succeed I would have to make sure that I had enough energy left over to stay ahead of him as the path was long and straight — there was little room for turning off in shame. Eventually, after running alongside him for about thirty seconds, I managed it. This man might have been seriously ill in his recent past. He might have had all sorts of problems I will never know about. But he was a man and he was about my age so it felt like a huge victory to be able to pass him.

That day in Salisbury I decided to try it again. I was sure that once we had passed the brow of that hill I would be able to make it. I steadied myself and then, as we descended, I tried to catch them. As I got closer I realised that the man on the right was describing the view to his companion. I assumed that it was some sort of concentration exercise. I had been known to count sheep or lamp-posts in the past. I slowed, my feet running in sync with theirs for a bit. The companion was barely replying, using mere grunts rather than words. Who was this rude man? Able-bodied, running with a mate and yet entirely ignoring him. I gave myself a little push and tried to get close enough to read the text on his running vest. Whichever snooty running club he was a member of would be one I'd be sure to give a swerve. Having accelerated a little I decided just to go for it and overtake them. I'd had enough of this strange dynamic, it was only going to irritate me if I carried on so close to them now.

As I drew up to overtake them I glanced to my right, poised to give this surly runner a sneer, to really let him know what I thought of the way he was treating his companion. He would never have seen me, because he barely had a face.

At first I thought that the sunlight was dappling shadow across his features. But no, he really did have only half a face. It was as I glanced at him, trying my best not to stumble in shock, that I saw the text on his vest was that of an army regiment. He was probably a veteran from the war in Afghanistan. And his injuries were profound. Where once there would have been eyes, there were only smooth scars. Likewise one of his ears. All of this above a body in perfect working condition. I swallowed and ran on, stunned by what I'd seen and ashamed of my knee-jerk assumptions.

Those mornings when I hadn't felt like going on runs, the days I'd had 'a bit of a head', the times I'd chosen to watch dross on TV instead of doing my stretches seemed ridiculous now. Here was a man half-destroyed by war, still choosing to push his body to the limit, while his mate described the scenery. I reached the finish line transfixed by thoughts of the opportunities I had and how little I made of them. It was a perfect boost to my training for the Brighton Marathon the following month, which I was now more committed to than ever.

9

Runner's High

'Stadiums are for spectators. We runners have nature and that is much better.'
Juha Vaatainen

If my first marathon had been about seeing if I could do it, and my second had been about helping a friend make a dream come true, my third was about finding out what I really was capable of. I wanted to know how far I could push myself, how fast I could go over a marathon distance and to discover how successfully I could harness my emotions to do this.

My ongoing battle to keep my body and mind working as partners was about to be challenged to its limits, not because of the distance, the practicalities of the race or the training schedule, but because I had no excuses. This time there was nowhere to hide. Running a marathon while harbouring no injuries, in my home town, was as simple as it could be. I had previously busied myself with attaching emotive monikers to my endeavours, from the 'lonely one' to the 'rage one', but this time I was going to approach the project like a machine. A marathon machine. A strong, controlled woman.

Things went better than I could have hoped. I trained hard throughout the spring, including a visit to the Lee Valley sports centre to watch what was to become Team GB training while I ran along the canal beside them, peering down from the towpath onto the athletics track below. I was disciplined about losing a bit of weight so that there was less Hemmo to carry along the course. I did my stretches, I worked hard with a trainer, the unfailingly patient Adam, to strengthen the muscles I needed most support from when running. I remained uninjured.

Gradually I relearned the lesson that I ran to improve my life; I didn't improve my life in order to be able to run. I ate better than I ever had, forcing myself to love oat smoothies under the tutelage of the former flatmate whose North London runs I had envied all those years ago. I took part in local park runs every Saturday and felt myself buoyed up by being part of a communal effort; I focused on fund-raising to make sure that for every aching muscle I suffered I was reminded that there were others in greater pain. I took resting seriously for the first time in my life

175

and didn't regret saying no to the odd night out, as I knew I was sleeping better than I ever had in my life. I moved house to the seafront and relished the admiration that the removal men expressed when I lifted almost the same amount as them and did it with ease. The routine propelled me forward, its comforting rhythm not numbing my mind with tedium but freeing it to be more creative in other areas than I ever had been. I ran along the seafront, I ran across the Downs, I ran myself the happiest I'd ever been. I was ready for the marathon.

Until tonsillitis. At first I just thought I was tired. Then I thought I had a sore throat. Next came the shivers. Two days before the marathon I showed my throat to a friend who took one look, shrieked and then announced, 'You look as if you have babies' anuses down there.' It was a low point.

The next day I tried calling my doctor to see if I could get an appointment. I spoke to her and she said she would leave me a prescription at the pharmacy, which I duly collected. Tonsillitis it was. My hopes of running a strong marathon were fading faster than I had ever run, but I wanted to know if I could at least still make the starting line. I didn't care if I ran a slow time now, but I still wanted to take part in the event I had been training six months for, the one that ran straight past my front door. All I was worried about was the possibility of doing myself lasting damage. In endurance running there is a fine line between gritty courage and downright dumb-ass bravado. I preferred to stay on the 'alive-er' side of that line. I tried calling my doctor again to ask whether I should run or not, but the surgery was now closed.

I put out a plea on Twitter in case there were any doctors online who could help. I received a barrage of answers about people having heart attacks and inflamed brains, along with plenty more terrifying scare stories that the Internet can provide someone who really doesn't need them. There was one useful tweet. A friend pointed me in the direction of Tim Weeks, a trainer who offered to call me. Moments later I was talking through my symptoms with him, as he is a hugely experienced runner and trainer, as well as being married to a GP.

'I don't mind it if it's hard, it's going to be hard anyway. I just don't want to be a fool and damage myself in the long term,' I explained.

'You won't do that with tonsillitis,' he reassured me.

'Are you sure? I have a lot of friends telling me not to run . . . '

'I am sure. But if you start you should do

so having accepted that you might not finish.'

'But that's the opposite of everything you are told about setting out for a marathon!'

'Yes, but you clearly have tonsillitis. You are in a weakened state. Just keep your chest covered for as long as you can when you start. And don't expect too much of yourself.'

The next morning I set off for Brighton's Preston Park with a long-sleeved top on and three scarves in my bag. As before, the feeling of handing over my bag left me with a slightly limbless sensation, as if I were missing more than just a few possessions. It was me and my body at the start line again, ready for another expedition into the unknown. When would I start a marathon knowing what was ahead? I wondered. I stared at my trainers on the grass below me and quietly chose to accept that maybe I never would.

The first half of the marathon was a breeze. I kept covered up for well over an hour and received a steady trickle of texts from friends, family and the lovely Tim Weeks. As we hit the seafront I saw Julia, waving like a maniac at me on the side of the road, and soon we had covered the distance of a half marathon. I received a text from my brother to say that he had just completed the Paris Marathon. I ran past the square in which I lived, I saw more friends and even my neighbours out on the street shouting and cheering. Then, at around mile twenty, I suddenly felt as if someone had pulled a stopper out of me. I had never eaten or trained better for a race in my life, but suddenly I felt utterly bloodless. It was something I had never felt before, even when I had hit the extremes of exhaustion. This wasn't just tiredness; it was a sort of refusal on my body's part to engage at all. I stopped at the next water station and took two drinks, which I drank while walking slowly at the side of the road. I gave myself a pep talk and decided to continue.

As with the London Marathon a large chunk of the second half of the course was in a large industrial space. It went past the Shoreham power station and a powerfully depressing sewage works. My brain was just looping now, telling me off for not having trained properly, for being weak, for not having the mental rigour to even get past the challenges it was setting itself. *You're just tired, you have an illness*, I kept trying to tell myself, only to have my own brain reply louder each time, reminding me of my own inadequacies. We plodded past iron gates and concrete wastelands while this hideous internal dialogue continued to torment me. *You're not good enough. It's not even that you're not good enough, it's that you can't even get any better. You're just not good.*

Eventually I couldn't take it any more and slowed to a walk, a heaving sob in the well of my stomach.

'You can't stop,' said a voice behind me.

I didn't turn around. I wasn't in the mood for people taking the piss.

'Seriously, you can't stop,' the voice repeated. 'You're the only thing keeping me going.'

I turned and saw a bloke about my age, running a couple of feet behind me. I raised my eyebrows at him. Well, I tried to. Even my eyebrows were exhausted.

'Honestly, I've been watching your feet and trying to keep mine in time with yours. It's the only thing that has kept me running since we were back there.' He waved a hand dismissively, suggesting that his opinion of a Sunday spent touring a sewage farm was as favourable as mine. 'If you stop running I will have to stop running, and I don't want to let my friend down.'

'Well, where is your friend?' I asked, dragging myself back into a run.

'He's gone ahead. But we were running this together for his mum.'

'Oh no, is she OK?'

'No, she died of cancer a few months ago, but I said I would run the marathon with him to raise money for the hospice where she was.'

'Oh.' I felt stilled. Perhaps my woes weren't quite that bad. 'I'm sorry.'

'It's OK, but really, you have to keep me running. I can't flake out now.'

'Yes, you're right, we really do have to keep running, don't we?'

'Yes.'

'Deal. I'm Alex.'

'And I'm Nick. Nice to meet you.' We shook hands.

'I won't leave you until this is done,' I said. 'And we'll run.'

Run we did. For the last five miles of that marathon we plodded along together, not fast, but not walking. I promised him for miles that there were friends at a house on the seafront, waiting to cheer us. It seemed like weeks until we got back to Hove, but when we did, what a greeting! They had made bunting! They were having an actual party! I waved and pointed at Nick, yelling, 'This is Nick!' until they all cheered for him too. As we approached the last mile his supporters did the same for me, and I beamed as his girlfriend caught his eye, tearfully proud.

As we finally got to the finish line, twenty-five minutes after the 4-hour 30-minute time I had been hoping to achieve, we had the kind of hug that you can only have with a total stranger you have shared an intense experience with. I had learned more about Nick in that last hour than I have ever found out about people I've worked with for years. I heard about his work rebuilding the *Cutty Sark*, and told him about running past it in the London Marathon. I told him about my family and he told me about the friend he was running to support. We had battled forwards, part of that collective endeavour to convert energy to money, to aid, to solace. We were making something bigger than salt, sweat and swollen feet. Only the two of us knew how horrible those last few miles had been, how spirit-crushing our own internal mechanisms can be and how sometimes it is only the hand of a stranger extended towards you that can get you to the very end. When we got there it was all the sweeter for it.

★　★　★

'I'll rest!' I promised my friends, who were by now muttering darkly about me overdoing things. And rest I did. I stayed at home in my deliciously ugly compression socks, eating whatever I wanted and catching up on ridiculous telly. When I was better I spent a month going to parties wearing silly heels. I enjoyed myself doing whatever I wanted, letting the routine's grip relax a little. I kept up with a few park runs and did some social runs with my sister who was now busy losing her baby weight running around the parks and commons of South London. I enjoyed the lack of pressure, the letting myself acquiese to the fact that no matter how hard you train, chasing a time or fund-raising target need not be the focus. My acceptance and enjoyment were a delight, and running brought me unmitigated gentle pleasures for months.

Then came the email. Edinburgh. I had forgotten about Edinburgh. During Part Two of my post-London Marathon madness one of the more 'fun' runs I had applied for was called 'The Speed of Light': a live running installation that was going to be part of the world-famous Edinburgh Arts Festival. I hadn't been convinced it would ever even happen — my perception of the Edinburgh Festival had always been tainted by that of the Fringe: a pub table of 22-year-old stoners trying to find a back room for some improv. Even if it was to take place I thought it would be much more about spectacle than any sense of athleticism. I'd forgotten about the event and most certainly forgotten about training for it. After all, it was four months after the Brighton Marathon. Until the morning I sat in bed with my laptop, some toast and peanut butter and a coffee, and saw the email. About training.

Whereas emails from the London Marathon usually arrive via the charity you are running for and are chatty blocks of text gearing you up for the challenge, this was a video. Of a man looking very angry on top of a hill. The man was Angus Farquhar, the organiser of the event, which was to comprise groups of runners in full-body light suits, running up and down Arthur's Seat in the dark, creating stunning visual effects for the spectators, who would be there on the hill watching live. I had been excited by the event, but now I was exhausted. And terrified.

The video began with a stern talk about how hill training was different from any other form of training, that if you could run ten miles confidently on the flat you still might struggle with the challenges that Arthur's Seat presented.

'Doing a few road runs will be a complete nightmare. You simply will not be able to keep the pace up, and keeping the pace up is essential,' warned Angus ferociously, as the wind came straight off the sea and ruffled his hair vigorously. 'If after ten minutes you need to walk your whole group will have to walk, and the whole beautiful effect of this work will be destroyed.'

Suddenly, running as art didn't feel like it was going to be that much fun. Angus spoke sternly of the type of training needed and of how we WOULD NOT COPE if we did not complete it. 'There is no magic to hill work, you just have to go out and train on hills.' Fair enough, but Angus, please, a smile would not hurt. There followed an even sterner talk about footwear. We were to buy proper trail shoes. Anyone in a regular pair of trainers was a fool, as good as taking their life into their own hands.

The camera focused again on Angus, looking increasingly livid. I could see from the ticker at the bottom of my screen that the missive was nearly over. A final word. 'I said we were on steep terrain, we are actually on the edge of a cliff, Salisbury Crags.' The camera panned past Angus to show a vertical drop of nearly fifty metres. 'But don't worry, we will never go within two metres of the cliff. It will be really easy to trip.'

Within two metres! With wind that stiff it didn't seem like very much at all. My heart rate had been rising steadily as the video progressed, until it was eventually at the rate it might have been had I just scaled the hill — sorry, mountain — itself. I forwarded the video to Adam my trainer with a bold 'LOL!' beneath it. But his response wasn't quite as chirpy, as the text that pinged back almost immediately announcing a sudden change in tactics revealed. I was going to have to up my running. Again. It was time to learn to run on rough terrain, and it was time to run at night. Again I guiltily kicked a new pair of heels under my bed and looked up some tips on hill training.

★   ★   ★

It was a full moon for my first night run on the South Downs. Adam and I had set out at 10 p.m., as early as we could have done given the late July weather. Dusk was falling as we drove out of Brighton, and by the time we set off from Devil's Dyke for Truleigh Hill the moon was almost directly above us. While I had grown to love runs after dark along the seafront I still gasped when we reached the top of the first hill and I looked out towards Brighton for the first time. The sea was visible even from here, the moon reflected in it. The scene was the sort of thing a Goth teenager might have on their bedroom wall, complete with a sympathetic yet masterful wolf at one side, howling. I was wearing my head lamp from the White Night Half Marathon and Adam was carrying a torch. The galloping sensation of running over chunks of chalk and flint was utterly different from the reliability of hitting tarmac or pavement. I could feel each of the muscles and bones in my foot pulling together, getting stronger and having a strange sort of fun as they tried to work out what they would hit with the next step. I felt my heart rate increase as I headed up and up, and I felt my body giggle as we juddered down a hill. I got home after midnight, grinning and excited. I didn't need to be scared; I was going to become art after all!

No matter how lofty my artistic ambitions had been they could not save me from the enormity of Arthur's Seat. I realised this as I walked towards it on the night of the event. It was a Saturday in mid-summer and as I headed through central Edinburgh it seemed as if the entire city was warming up for the mother of all parties. I paced through the streets in my nerdy little trail shoes and merino-wool running top, past bars humming with the nervous energy and still-lipglossed hope of a good Saturday night. I headed out of the city and to the tiny city of marquees at the bottom of the hill. We were gathered in groups and then walked out onto the hill to be given a run-through of our routines. We would be running in circles, zigzags and other patterns across the landscape, wearing our light suits like wannabe spacemen, and holding special torches that lit up when shaken. Excitement bubbled through the group and I felt a flicker of smugness at those I had passed on the way. Pah! I was going to be the one having the magical Saturday night after all!

Dusk was falling and a TV in a corner of one of the marquees was broadcasting the final Saturday night of the Olympics, as Angus appeared to give us a pep talk about the event. He began with some characteristically stern words about how the environment up on Arthur's Seat is 'very serious at night'. 'It can turn on you,' he told us with gravitas. 'The terrain is rough and the mist can come in just like that.' I stifled a nervous giggle. Then, as he talked more about the event, I found myself becoming converted to its magic. Running is a generous act, he explained, and the energy we were creating would be helping to power the light suits and the torches. Our movement would be translated into light to be shared and enjoyed by others. He even cracked a smile at the end.

Eventually at about 11 p.m. we set out for the hill. The light suits were heavier than I had expected, covering our arms, legs and torsos. As we began to run, slowly, steadily but always in formation, I felt a sort of euphoria coming over me. As we approached each craggy hill I felt a thrill as I realised my legs and heart were more than strong enough to keep me constant regardless of the terrain. I had the power to go uphill when led and not to gallop away when we headed downhill. I heard animals in the undergrowth, I heard the gasps of the audience as we burst into little star shapes of energy on the side of the hill, I heard the panting of the ten of us in my group, running on in silence. A whole new world of running seemed to be opening up to me, one where goals, times and distances were not important, but just running across a landscape and feeling it underfoot was enough.

As I walked back to my hotel through the now rather tired-looking streets of Edinburgh I tried to see myself through the eyes of those who had come to watch the event. What sort of person does that? they must surely have been thinking. It was undeniably beautiful, but also a sort of madness. I tried to see myself through the eyes of my friends and family who had been watching my progress all year. What is she up to? they must have been wondering. Running was no longer how I stayed fit but who I was. It was how I functioned, how I relaxed, how I processed my emotions. It was something that those who loved me, loved *about* me.

10

The Right to Run

'Running gives freedom. When you run you can determine your own tempo. You can choose your own course and think whatever you want. Nobody tells you what to do.'

Nina Kuscik

Oh, how I felt magnificent as I sat there on the train back from Edinburgh. As the gorgeous voluptuousness of the Cumbrian hills whizzed by I actually felt as if I were part of them. My running had melded me with the landscape all over again. I stared at the cleavage of a valley, knowing what the gentle give of the turf felt like beneath my feet. My eyes softened as we passed a lake and I remembered the glassy water of the Firth of Forth as I stared out over Edinburgh in the middle of the night. I had never enjoyed running more, never felt more part of something, as though running alone was the destination rather than a personal best or a fund-raising target.

Like an evangelical recent non-smoker, I just wanted to preach the benefits of My Way to everyone I knew. I would do this, I decided. I would no longer be the woman who just encouraged those who already knew they wanted to run — I would convert them all! I would create a nation of runners, strong and proud! Then I fell asleep until Wolverhampton, my feet gently throbbing in my trainers.

As the train pulled into Euston I felt my almost hallucinatory dreams of converting the world to running supremacy gently fade. *It's understandable*, I told myself. *You were bound to feel a little high after an event like that. Just focus on the training for San Francisco — two months to go!*

But, somehow, that didn't happen.

The excitement for running hills had blunted the once-reliable pleasure of endurance training for me. I felt excuses not to run slowly coil round my steadfastness like ivy creeping up a solid house. I knew I could run a marathon, why stress myself out about this one? Was the point not proven now? I wanted to spend time with baby Louis before he was running himself. I wanted to see more of my London friends, feeling bad for not making it to parties on the nights before big races. I wanted the goals I was setting myself to simply stop shifting. Meanwhile I was falling in love and hauling myself out of bed on a Sunday morning was no longer simply about tiredness but leaving someone behind.

But I did it anyway and plodded along the seafront in a sort of daze. *Oh WELL DONE, the tide*, a sulky voice would say in my head, like a recalcitrant teenager. *You're not as good as a MASSIVE VALLEY though, are you?* My running times slumped. When I felt I was almost sprinting I was barely completing a 5km run as fast as I had been able to nine months earlier. Seams I never knew existed on my running clothes started to irritate. My hair would flap in my face until I was convinced I'd fall off the pier, blinded. My necklace tangled in the cord of my headphones. And I was sure I was always running into the wind.

Perhaps, I found myself thinking, running was just something I had done to fill a void. Maybe it was just a pastime for the lonely, to give a shape and purpose to their empty nights and weekends. It could just have been a way to brag all along — a cunning disguise for elaborate attention-seeking. Now that all areas of my life were so much happier it seemed like little more than indulgence, an unnecessary purgatory that I had inflicted on myself. What had once held a certain nobility now seemed almost pathetic. If that were the case, perhaps I no longer needed it.

The thought solidified inside of me, a crackling crust forming round my misgivings. A shiver ran through me. I shoved these doubts as far back in my mind as I could. I half-heartedly reassured myself that everyone felt a dip in enthusiasm from time to time, not just those in love. I continued to plod along the seafront, shaving one or two seconds off my time, but little more. My determination to achieve a personal best in my next marathon seemed to be dragged further away with every passing tide. And the idea of running after it seemed to be drifting even further.

'The only way to run a faster marathon is to get used to running faster,' Adam my trainer told me when I went to see him, huffing with indignation that my legs seemed to be refusing to run any faster. He assured me that the books were right — sprint training, shorter faster distances were what I needed to be focusing on. I already knew I had the endurance. But I hated sprint training; it was everything that had put me off running for all of those years in the first place. The aggressive, leonine competitive instinct that requires you to run *as fast as you possibly can*, turning your mind to nothing but speed and pain — it repulsed me. The

193

whole experience served only to remind me of those very first runs, when every single judder of my arse felt like my own body taunting me.

I could just about tolerate heading up and out of Brighton to the pretty Withdean athletics track, pretending I was Jessica Ennis or Steve Prefontaine as I attempted to hurtle across the terracotta-coloured tartan, which is the ridiculous name for the substance the track is made of. But when I was tasked with sprint training alone I filled with purest despair. It is one thing to master the mental sleight of hand required to dress in tight Lycra and run in public, but to sprint up and down the seafront, thirty seconds or one hundred metres at a time — it feels like asking for scorn. Not built like a sprinter I knew I looked like someone trying too hard, someone reaching beyond their capabilities, or — worst of all — someone showing off. There was none of the pleasure of running and all of the pain. I swallowed hard and tried to pretend I didn't think this, still smilingly answering questions from friends and colleagues about my latest running adventures and trying to keep motivation high in anyone who asked me about their own endeavours. With every passing day I felt like more of a fraud.

'What is it you are running from?' a friend asked me when I said I wouldn't be able to make a Sunday lunch he was arranging because I would be doing a half marathon.

'I don't know,' I replied, flummoxed by the question. Was I running from something? It had never occurred to me that I was.

'You can't run from yourself, you know,' he said with a wry smile. I tried to focus on his paunch and the woollen tank top stretched across it.

'Oh, I know,' I said. 'Me just keeps popping up at the finish line, wherever I run.'

Had I got away with it? Or had he sensed that I was starting to not believe in myself? I think I was. That question haunted me though. Whereas a month previously I had felt so proud of my strength and leanness I now felt my own paunch mount a slight return, the result of lazy love-struck afternoons spent at the pub instead of haring along the seafront. I couldn't work out what I was running for any more, let alone what I was running from. Maybe I was over-thinking it. The simple fact was: I couldn't be arsed any more. Was it too late to pull out of San Francisco? My eyes drifted around my bedroom looking for something to trip over. You can't argue with injury.

I kept these thoughts to myself for as long

as I could. I posted the photographs of my Edinburgh experience online and lapped up the interest and enthusiasm from others. Yet it did little or nothing to reinvigorate me. I thought if I bottled it up the feeling would pass, it would dissolve, spore-like into the atmosphere. But bottling things up turned out to be as much one of my skills as sprinting is.

One August weekend I went to a friend's birthday dinner, a party I'd been looking forward to for weeks. I knew that there would be my favourite people in attendance, bundles of good food and lots to drink. As I sat there and looked around the room I realised it was exactly the sort of thing I had hoped I'd be doing by the time I was in my mid-thirties. An enormous sense of contentment came over me, one with a dash of luminous smugness running through it, like in a stick of Brighton rock. This is it, I have achieved adulthood splendidly, I thought to myself.

There were about fifteen of us, all seated at makeshift tables composed of various people's garden furniture. It was the prettiest dining hall in Brighton, candles flickering and glasses of Prosecco being raised at regular intervals in a flurry of congratulations, celebrations and happy birthdays. Two huge serving dishes of lobster macaroni cheese were brought to the table, complete with elegant pink lobster claws poking from their tops. We gasped in excitement and a dish was held in front of me. I reached for the serving spoon on the table and dolloped a huge, rosy chunk on my plate, emboldened by the booze I'd already had.

'Why not? It's a party!' I said, as I realised quite how much I had served myself. I hastily passed on the dish.

'I suppose when you run as much as you do you can have as much as you want!' said a friend of a friend who was sitting opposite me.

'Well, exactly!' I said chirpily, vowing never to let on how little running I had been doing recently.

'How is it going anyway?' asked another friend, her eyes twinkling with enthusiasm. I sensed a threat. This was someone who had previously asked for my advice on running. The food was now making its way from plates to mouths. I mumbled a non-committal reply, hoping that my friend wouldn't notice. No one was listening anyway, they were probably as bored as I was by the whole thing. And she probably hadn't even stuck with the running.

'I'm sorry?' she said, assuming she had not heard me on account of the general hubbub in the room.

Something inside snapped. I couldn't fake it any more. My hand flopped down onto the table, hitting it far harder than I had intended, causing cutlery to jangle in unison and wine glasses to tinkle against each other. Silence. Heads slowly turned towards me.

'I'm just so bloody BORED of running!' I said, far too loudly for a now largely silent room. 'I mean, what's the fucking POINT?' I raised my Prosecco to my mouth and as I peered over the edge of the glass defiantly I saw several sets of eyes staring back at me, concerned. The secret was out.

'Oh, that's a shame,' said my friend. 'It used to make you so happy. You even got me into it!'

'Why, are you . . . not enjoying it?' another friend asked, timidly.

I rolled my eyes dramatically.

'I just can't see the point any more,' I declared with a curled lip. 'I know I can run a marathon, I know I can get to Saltdean and back when it's raining, I know I beat a lot of people my age and I know I will always be beaten by a lot of others. I don't need any of this. Why should I be trying sooo hard to get twenty minutes faster? What's the purpose? What would I ever do with that extra twenty minutes?'

I waved an arm drunkenly, possibly at

some imaginary trainer in the room.

'I don't have to run far to find berries, I don't have to run fast to escape tigers. I just don't need to run. I can't work out why I ever bothered really,' I continued. I was on a roll now, unplugged, I seemed unable to stop.

Silence.

'I know, I know, it's awful.'

'It's not awful,' ventured a voice. 'It's just a bit of a shame. You were so passionate about it.'

'I don't know why I have been trying so hard — I'm never going to win, so why am I so concerned by getting faster?'

'That never seemed to be why you were doing it though. You always spoke about how happy it made you in other ways. It never seemed that much about speed.'

I shrugged and scooped a second helping of lobster macaroni cheese onto my plate, willing the focus to shift from me.

'Which marathon is it that you are training for now?' piped up another voice, a friend's husband.

'The Nike Women's Marathon.'

'And where's that?' someone else chipped in.

'In San Francisco.'

'Oh wow! That is my favourite city in the world.' Nearly the whole table was looking at me now.

'Yes, I have wanted to go for years,' I replied. 'The race starts really early so you see the sun rise over the Golden Gate Bridge. I've wanted to do it for a long time.'

'That sounds fantastic!'

'What an experience!'

'It must be such an amazing way to see a city — they close all the roads for you and people cheer you on, like visiting royalty!'

'Yes, yes it is.' My voice was smaller now.

'If you can do that why would you even bother about how fast you can do it?'

'I suppose I need a sense of . . . progression.'

'So you see getting faster as the mark of progression rather than enjoying the experience more?'

'Well, yes, yes I suppose I do.'

* * *

When I woke up the next morning, groggy from booze and mildly shamed by my churlish outburst, I wondered again why I had fallen out of love with running with such a thud. Was it the pressure of chasing times again? Was it that I thought I didn't need it any more? And why should I need to do something in order to deem it worthwhile? For the first time in months I thought I'd try to solve a running dilemma the old-fashioned way: I emailed my dad. The subject header: 'I just don't seem to be able to get any faster at running!'

His reply was succinct to say the least: 'Why do you want to move fast when you are training for a marathon? Fast is relative.'

When I explained my frustrations, how I felt I was running in treacle, how I wasn't sure I could be bothered any more, a similar reply came back: it's not always about the time, it's about the experience, about how you feel when you're out there.

He was right. Of course he was. I decided not to think about times, to abandon the ceaseless maths project of working out paces and applying them to miles and kilometres. This in turn freed up some mental space for me to think about other things while I was running, instead of endlessly checking my pace. Most crucially it freed up space in my mind to try and enjoy the act of running once more.

For the final few weeks of training I made a real effort to relax, to relish every step, to look forward to the process not the destination. To feel my feet pushing the ground away from me, not feel my knees reaching forward. I got up one Sunday to run the Hove 10k along the seafront and stunned myself by completing it four minutes faster than ever before and being in good enough shape afterwards to enjoy six oysters with the man I had left sleeping ninety minutes earlier. Perhaps there was space for my love affair with running as well as other affairs of the heart after all.

Then, out of the blue, after years of following her career I was given the chance to interview Paula Radcliffe at an event being held by her sponsors Nike on Clapham Common. I arrived huffing and out of breath in the clammy summer heat. A crowd had already gathered to see her interviewed on the stage. As she walked out I saw that she was with sprinter Carl Lewis. My heart was in my throat. The eight-year-old me that had been entranced by Olympic Lewis's prowess in the 1984 Olympics wondered what my dad would think of me seeing him in person now.

The two of them were interviewed on stage then Paula waded through crowds of fans asking her to sign things, to speak to them, to meet their babies. Eventually I was taken to the press area. As a result of my enthusiasm, I was to be allowed to interview both of the stars. I was, however, warned that they would be brief and I quickly prepared myself. I sat down to speak to Carl — a genuine icon. He was glowing and I basked in his beam, overawed. His trainers were box fresh and his running jacket was silver reflective fabric. He shone in a way that only the very healthy or very rich can do. He was immaculately polite and listened very carefully to my questions. I asked him what he would advise the woman who thought she might like to become a runner, but had no idea how. The woman who still believed that there was a secret that needed unlocking. Who felt that she needed permission from someone.

Mr Lewis gave me a very long, involved answer about how that woman should pick a route or a distance she wanted to run, and then to walk it every day for a month. He was convinced that this woman would then feel her 'natural competitiveness' surge within and break into a run, desperate to move at speed. I nodded, smiling. I could kind of see his point, but inside there was a clear voice, one that was not wearing a silver jacket, that said, 'I'm not sure that any woman would see that through. She would have told herself she was wasting everyone's time halfway through week two. She would never make it to running.

I thanked Mr Lewis, choking back emotion as I explained how much it would mean to my dad that I'd spoken to him. But deep down I knew I wouldn't be passing his advice on to anyone beyond my male running friends. I held out for Paula though. Paula would have the answer. Surely the most iconic long-distance runner of our time would provide me with the solid gold nugget of advice that I could in turn pass on to generations of would-be runners. I would be enthused anew! A nation of runners would be born! Inspire a generation!

Paula was unfailingly polite as she ever is. Somehow I neglected to tell her about my recent and dramatic decline in enthusiasm, and pretended that all of my questions were for the novice runner. I asked her the same question — what would she recommend for that would-be runner?

There was a gentle pause before Paula answered softly, 'Just go out and run. Just . . . go out and try it. That is the easiest way to get involved, to get hooked and to experience what it can bring to your life. Do it. Go out and have fun, see if you like it.'

'Yes, yes of course,' I mumbled politely. We chatted some more and I thanked her profusely, before heading for the Tube, somewhat despondent.

'Never meet your heroes,' was ringing in my ears as I boarded the train to Brighton. It had all been a bit of a waste of time really. Neither of them had given me that fresh perspective on running that I had been searching for since Edinburgh. I began to wonder if it would ever happen. Once home I listlessly Googled a couple of the names that Paula had mentioned in our chat: Ingrid Kristiansen, whom she had watched break the world record in 1985, trailblazing Norwegian runner Grete Waitz, and Joan Benoit Samuelson. I'd heard of her. She was the first woman to win the Olympic gold for the marathon. But it was only then that I learned that it wasn't an Olympic event for women until 1984. I decided to find out more.

Three hours later I was still pinned to my laptop, slack-jawed at what I was discovering. There were these women, these incredible women, who had been fighting to run competitively for decades. As recently as the 1960s they had been told that they couldn't, that they wouldn't, and that they mustn't. There were women who had been forcibly removed from races when they'd chosen to run alongside men and not be counted, who had defied society and tradition to be allowed to run. And they weren't tedious gym bunnies or brainlessly competitive automatons. They had been rock stars of the road in their time and then gone on to become doctors and mathematicians. And there was I, a little cheesed off with the prospect of running a few times a week.

The next morning I went for a run, chastened by what I had read. My head was swimming with my discoveries. These women weren't running to keep fit, to stay slim or to impress anyone but themselves. They weren't chasing approval but chasing the effervescent joy of running. They were running to run, just as Paula had suggested. As I turned off the seafront and headed for home I realised that Paula had been right after all. Sometimes, to find out if you are a runner, you just have to go out and run. And it turned out that I still was.

11

The Finish Line

'Only those who will risk going too far can possibly find out how far one can go . . . '
T. S. Eliot

I closed the hotel room door behind me and burst into tears. I was terrified. I opened my bag, got out my father's 25-year-old Helly Hansen woollen running top and threw it on the bed, desperately hoping it might emit a bit of courage back at me. Apparently not. I was going to have to find a bit of my own. I unpacked forlornly and looked at the contents of the cupboard when I was done. Two pairs of trainers. A pair of tracksuit bottoms. Two pairs of running tights. Two running tops. And a dress. An unusual selection when you looked at it laid out like that. But then my friends had been telling me all year that it was quite unusual to spend so much time trying to get to the other side of the world to go for a run with a load of women you've never met. And I'd still gone and done that. I reached for my trainers.

Eleven hours earlier the plane left the ground and the Thames gradually got smaller beneath us. Even though I could still see it London suddenly seemed very far away. San Francisco seemed even further away. The city had existed for so long as a sort of holy grail in my mind. The Brighton of the United States, it was the city built on Gold Rush money and designed for having fun in. Fantastic food, beautiful scenery and of course the majestic Golden Gate Bridge, which had transfixed me since childhood.

Seeing down over the bridge had been a big part of the reason I wanted to run the Nike Women's Marathon and now I was finally going to get to do it. I was going to run San Francisco, surrounded by women. I was so nervous at the thought that I burst into tears and sat in a bit of a daze for the first hour of the flight, scrolling through my most recent photographs of those most beloved to me. Eventually I calmed myself down enough to sleep a while, but as I got to the hotel and realised just how alone I was, how far from everyone I knew and loved, I felt rigid with terror and utterly weak.

Sleep was fitful. The next day I had arranged to go for a run with some other British runners I had got in touch with in the weeks before. We headed out from Union

Square, where the marathon HQ was, and down to the Embarcadero, the road running alongside the water. It was 9 a.m., although my brain was still convinced it was something else entirely. Both the water and the October sky were a perfect clear blue. My eyes widened as I caught sight of a bridge ahead of me, only to realise that it was not the right one. We continued along the water, past the farmers' market now opening up, local artists setting up stalls, and boats delivering fish to the restaurants. I felt my heart swell with emotion again, only this time not as a result of despair and anxiety, but excitement. I had made it! I was in San Francisco, where I had wanted to be for so long, and I had got there through running!

My stride lengthened and I felt the cramps and tightness from the flight dissolving away. I stretched my arms out in front of me and took a deep breath. As I grinned at the city around me I slightly convinced myself I had actually run there. I certainly felt tired enough. When I closed the hotel door behind me the next time I was smiling, feeling lighter. Running had done that.

Later that morning I was invited to a press breakfast where we were introduced to the athlete Allyson Felix. A superstar Olympian of 2012, she was one of the many magnificent women who had graced our TV screens over the summer, looking strong, proud and goddess-like. To be in this room with her, to sit and chat with one of the women who had helped promote the idea that a useful body, a strong body, might be of more value than a merely decorative one, was amazing. Once again I was star-struck. I asked her about distance running and she said she'd never run further than four miles, and anyone who had was, as far as she was concerned, 'someone with a great gift'.

How had the simple act of putting one leg in front of the other made this possible? How was I now living out the dreams of the little me on the sofa, legs dangling, unable to touch the carpet, watching the man soaring across the stadium in the jet pack at the 1984 Los Angeles Olympics? I felt more complete than I ever had, more back to my me-est me than I had done for so long. Those weeks of despair during training seemed to melt away. I had a gift, I repeated to myself. I had a gift.

I wasn't feeling quite as gifted the next morning when my alarm went off at 4.30 a.m. I put on my running kit, laid out as usual on the floor by the end of the bed. I rubbed Vaseline all over my feet, remembering that first time my father had told me to do so and how I had scoffed at him. I necked a cup of coffee and a carton of coconut water, my favourite pre- and post-run drink, full of electrolytes and far superior to those glucose drinks in my opinion. I headed out through the reception of the hotel, where the concierge waved and wished me luck.

Union Square was still swathed in darkness, but there was a buzz in the warm air. The area had been taken over by the marathon since I'd arrived, but now there was a certain vibe that let me know that it was time for real business. The huge palm trees were twinkling with fairy lights in the darkness. There were security fences going up around the now-closed roads and several streets were lined with big yellow American school buses, ready to bring the runners home from the finish line.

I crossed the square and headed to an all-night diner where a group of us had arranged to meet. I had some toast and eggs, my usual marathon breakfast, while we took it in turns to go to the bathroom and fix our race numbers to our tops. Crowds were starting to gather, like a sort of running zombie nation in the half-light. As ever I found myself marvelling at the myriad shapes and sizes of the runners. In among the crowd there were a few men, but all of them had marked themselves out as either survivors of or those left bereft by the cancer whose charity the marathon was in association with.

Within half an hour I had joined the throng standing in the streets, lined up and ready to begin. I could just about see the stage, where my new heroine Joan Benoit Samuelson took the microphone and declared the start. I was going to be running in the same race as her. I was thrilled as the crowds inched forward slowly as daylight started to appear. Moments later we set off amidst whoops and cheers and copious well-wishing.

We headed to the edge of the bay and ran north towards the Golden Gate Bridge. The crowd fell largely silent, the thump of runners' feet the loudest sound around us. As the water lapped against the harbour I could smell the fish and wondered how far they had all swum. I tried to remember the route map that I had studied for so long back at home in Brighton and then on the plane. I had a pang of longing for home. Then I remembered the bridge. We were going to be there soon, weren't we?

Well, yes, we were, but so was something else. A mist, the likes of which I'd never seen before. It was thick and claggy, and coming straight off the water. I could feel the humidity settling in my lungs every time I breathed in. I looked around me and saw how much my visibility had been reduced. It now looked as if there were only a few runners around me, not the hundreds I knew I had set off with. Had it not been for the neon splashes on the odd running vest I would scarcely have believed I was doing what I was. Fear crept back in. Would the whole run be like this? How would I know where I was going? The marks on the map that I had memorised were suddenly obsolete now that I could see no distance at all.

Then I realised we were running past the bridge — the Golden Gate of my dreams! And all I could see of it was two concrete stumps, looming above the water. It was still very early on in the race and a crushing sense of dispiritedness was starting to consume me. How would I cope if the whole race were like this, so different from everything I had anticipated?

The delicate fabric that was holding my confidence together began to unravel. I wasn't sure if I'd make it without the visual and emotional treats I had bribed myself with. But then suddenly the landscape changed, distracting me altogether. A hill appeared, a huge hill. Five months of my breezy tweets in reply to anyone who had asked about the hills of San Francisco suddenly seemed rather facetious. I thought of my passion for hill running that summer and I imagined that enthusiasm pushing me up the hill. And what a reward was waiting when I got there! There was a spectacular view down across what water was visible. No bridge, but as our heads were literally up above the mist and clouds, I felt something approaching invincibility.

I gasped, not just out of breathlessness but excitement. This route was proving to be as astonishing as I had hoped. The views continued to be more and more spectacular as the mist cleared. I felt like an explorer, understanding the drive to seek out the unknown and push myself to the limit. There was also the drive to see really cool houses like the one that Sharon Stone's character has in *Basic Instinct*, sitting on her deck, staring moodily into the woods.

As the halfway point approached, those in the crowd who were running the half marathon started to peel away, turning towards their finish line and leaving the rest of us to do the final thirteen-mile loop. I wasn't even halfway done, but a certain loneliness was starting to creep over me at seeing so many runners turn away. Although the distance I'd covered from Union Square felt endless, the remaining distance to the finish line seemed unfathomable. I longed for a running partner, a teammate, a companion of some sort.

Then came the texts. I had entirely forgotten about it, but Nike had created an app which meant that my Facebook page could chart my progress with messages I had prepared in advance. When I crossed the mats at certain milestones the chip on my shoe was activated and Facebook loaded a message updating where I was. It was a more sophisticated version of the system that Adidas had implemented all those years ago when I had run my first London Marathon. A pre-running Julia had followed me on her old Nokia and sent me text updates for three hours. This time, although the system had been updated, the need for it had not. My heart surged as the messages started to appear.

'You are not alone, we are here with you.'

'Hemmo! A branch of John Lewis might be opening in Hove! Run home soon!'

'KEEP GOING, DARLING!'

Suddenly a photograph of Louis appeared, wagging his hands excitedly at the camera, wearing a snazzy pair of tracksuit bottoms. I wanted to hug my phone.

Next a simple row of kisses arrived. I was not alone. I never was and I never would be.

My spirits lifted. I waved goodbye to the

half marathoners and looked around me at the women who were left. It was unusual for me not to be surrounded by fancy dress characters or slower runners at this point in a marathon. This time the other women were just like me. They weren't freaks or hard-bodied obsessives, or slaves to the track. They were women trying their hardest. Wearing photos of their family who inspired them. They were inspiring each other. We would run together.

We turned into Prospect Park at mile eleven and I looked around me at the natural beauty, stunned that I had made it here, that I was actually allowed to run this course. We passed waterfalls, unfamiliar tree types and even a field of buffalo. After a few more loops we came to the seafront again. There were waves lapping onto the beach at the side of the highway. The sea looked so infinite, so inspiring.

But as the miles passed I began to feel the ache of the distance I had run and started to feel drained by the effort. The flight, the homesickness and the miles yet to come all seemed to be rushing at me. A wooziness came over me and I gripped my phone tighter, willing some more messages to make their way to me. Once again I felt far away from home and desperately lonely. But I kept going, one foot in front of the other, one foot in front of the other, keep in time with the waves, keep a beat with the sea. My energy was ebbing with the tide and slowly, slowly, I felt myself lapse into a walk.

'No, darling, no!' said a voice to my right. I turned and the face of a small, wiry woman, maybe twenty years older than me, was smiling up at mine.

'Sorry,' I mumbled.

'You don't walk, darling!'

'I don't think I can go on, I just feel so tired.'

'No, darling, keep going, I'm with you.' She had a strong South American accent so I asked her where she was from.

'El Salvador, darling, but I run all over the world.'

'Wow, really? This is the first time I've run abroad. How many marathons have you done?'

'Fifty! All over the world! I love to run.'

Her smile seemed as broad as the beach itself. Yet I still felt horrendous. I thought perhaps I was going to be sick as water started to course down the inside of my mouth, in a way I had only previously experienced after a teenage night of too much cider.

'Come on, darling, it's less than two miles. We're going to do it. You and me. You are so special. What's your name?'

'Alexandra.'

'Alexandra! Like Alexandra the Great! You are so special, keep going, keep going.'

I was swallowing hard now, trying to keep myself from being sick. I seemed to be seeing things in black and white as my vision blurred. Was this Hitting The Wall? Wasn't that meant to be earlier in a race? Why was I suddenly . . . so . . . very . . . tired?

My eyes opened with a start as I felt her grip my hand.

'We are nearly there, Alexandra! Look at the colours! Let's keep looking at the colours. Look at the yellow shorts. Can you see the bright yellow? Wonderful! Oooooh my! Look at her socks! Pink knee socks, well I never! See the sky, Alexandra, see how blue the sky is now. Keep going, keep going.'

And so she continued, holding my hand, coaxing me on like a child. I looked at the colours. I loved her. I wanted to be at home.

'Look, Alexandra! We are nearly at the end! There will be firemen there. And necklaces. You are going to make it. You are so wonderful, such a special girl. Look at the colours, keep your legs steady, here we are.'

I saw the balloons that marked the finish line and just stared until I reached them, willing myself forward with force of will alone. It seemed that someone had kicked me behind the knees. As the balloons grew closer the relief was so intense that I could barely keep myself upright.

'Thank you so much thank you so much thank you so much,' I sobbed, holding her hand tighter than ever. And finally we crossed the line, holding hands above our heads. I collapsed into the arms of one of the many tuxedo-clad firemen and accepted the Tiffany's box he handed me on a silver platter. My marathon prize was not a medal this time but a necklace. I grabbed my friend and some of the others I had finished alongside, and wept. We had made it. Look at the colours. I would be home soon. Home.

★　★　★

Sitting in the departure lounge at the airport the next day I felt my phone ping, announcing an email. I recognised the name in my inbox, but in my exhaustion I couldn't quite place it: Kathrine Switzer. I opened the message and only as I read it through for the second time did I realise who it was from. Another of my marathon heroes, this time congratulating me on my marathon time. I had written to her months before to request an interview and only now had she had the chance to reply. But, as a fellow runner, she knew how much it would mean to me to look up my time and congratulate me first. What had been disappointment at an unimproved speed turned to pride. What a woman. The tears prickled in my eyes again and moments later my flight was called.

It was only three days since I had left London but I felt I now knew myself better than I had done in the whole year before I had left. I now knew that I was a runner for life. No matter what else was going on around me, no matter how long the gaps between my runs, no matter how high, how long or how fast my races were, I was a runner. Once you have taught yourself that running isn't about breaking boundaries you thought you could never smash, and realised that it is about discovering those boundaries were never there in the first place, you can apply it to anything.

I sat in my seat on the plane, gazing out of the window at the bay below, and put my hand up to touch my necklace medal. Was that the Golden Gate Bridge we were flying over? I stared hoping, until we were above the ocean. I flicked through some notes I had taken with me and found a quote I had scribbled down. It was Julia Chase-Brand talking about her famous road race, the only woman among a sea of men. 'Finishing that race was a defining moment for me. If I could handle that pressure, I realized I could go ahead and live my life as I wanted. I could do anything.'

I finally knew what she meant. The races, the quiet solitary runs, the ridiculous rainy ones with friends. They all involved shifting a bit of blood around and getting my legs to take me from one place to the next, but they had also been about so much more: the shame overcome, the courage discovered and the exhilaration reached. Running had made my heart bigger, but only now did I understand in how many ways.

It is about having the determination to try and exceed your expectations, and the strength to accept that sometimes you might not. It is having the insight to know which are the friends who will stand in the raging heat or icy rain just to catch a glimpse of you that will lift your spirits for miles to come. It is the deepening of family bonds you never even knew you had. It is the discipline to stick to what you need to do to get where you need to go. It is the courage to leave someone you love in a warm bed, hoping that they will still love you when you return an hour later, sweating and cross. It is the stalwart belief of others who tell you that you can do it when you are certain you can't, and the gift of telling others that very same thing when they suffer their own self-doubt. It is reaching out to a total stranger who might need help — whether they are suffering on the track beside you or in a hospital bed on the other side of the world. It is about defying convention, choosing who you are and taking the initiative to become that person. It is a hug from a stranger and total understanding from those you love the most.

Running makes you big-hearted.

PART 2

That was my story, and this part shall be about making it yours. Here are the answers to the queries I tormented myself with when I learned to run, as well as some extra ones I have been asked over the years since. I was lucky to have my father for advice, but there were some questions he just couldn't deal with. I have been that woman typing 'What happens when you run with big boobs?' into the search bar in the dead of night, and I have spent more hours than I care to count in running shops and at event expos, trying to work out what certain pieces of kit are actually for. Here is what I have found on my adventures.

Running style, fear of injury, and mystifying kit: it's all here. There is only one thing I could not find a solution to, and that is getting your period on the day of a big event. In running as in life, sometimes it just happens — it's down to you to get on with it. Lots of tampons, lots of painkillers and the certainty that those post-race carbs will taste even better are all yours for the taking. Keep your head high and run like a girl.

12

The Women in Whose Tracks We Run

'Running is the greatest metaphor for life, because you get out of it what you put into it.'

Oprah Winfrey

Dr Julia Chase-Brand

'I feel more like myself when I'm out running. I'm a good animal.'

Dragging yourself out of bed for a muddy race on a frosty morning rarely feels like a luxury. But it is one that the women of the 1960s and 1970s were not afforded. Unbelievably, fit, healthy and enthusiastic women were being turned away from public races as recently as a few decades ago. Repeatedly warned that they were too weak, they defiantly refused to be told they could not run, even when forcibly removed from the field, disqualified or ignored. These are their stories, and in whose steps we tread, once we

227

have laced our trainers.

Julia Chase-Brand grew up in Connecticut, USA, running through the woods surrounding her grandmother's farm. She wasn't running to keep fit or to lose weight, but because she enjoyed how it felt — the speed, the weightlessness, the sensation that flying might only be a few steps away. But this childhood passion, which had turned serious by her late teens, was stopped in its literal tracks in 1960. The Amateur Athletic Union prohibited women from competing in official road races. This was not just a quirk of the Union — it went as far as the Olympics, where it was forbidden for women to take part in public races of further than half a mile for fear of the risk to their femininity and reproductive health. There were even officials who warned that distance running could cause the uterus to fall out. When Julia showed up for the 1960 Manchester Road Race she was denied entry.

By 1961 organisers were more sympathetic: women could now take part. There were two minor conditions though: their results would not count and they could not run with the men. Effectively they were allowed to run along behind, with little heed taken of their times. By now Julia had been attending Olympic trials nationally and had unofficially entered a road race in Massachusetts where she had finished ahead of eight men. She decided to give the Manchester race another go. She filed her application and made no secret of the fact that she had every intention of defying the AAU restrictions on women.

Chase-Brand's grandmother Mary Foulke Morrisson was a suffragette, her great-grandfather William Dudley Foulke was president of the American Woman Suffrage Association. And Julia's steeliness also extended beyond her running abilities. She wasn't just going to turn up for the race and take part, she was going to do it as the very best and proudest woman she could be.

The media were intrigued by her and followed her story with an uneasy mixture of support and patronising headlines and questions, from 'She Wants to Chase the Boys' to 'Women don't run. You run. What are you?' They were flummoxed by her unapologetic combination of strength and femininity. How could a 'girl' so funny, so pretty, also be so full of grit? 'Under questioning, Miss Chase said she is 5'4.5, weighs 118 lbs and does not know her other dimensions. (Eyewitnesses report her other dimensions are very good),' said the *New York Journal-American* only a week before the race.

She turned up on the day looking stridently

feminine, regardless of the restrictions she knew would be placed upon her. 'I wasn't masquerading as a male,' Chase-Brand said. 'I was what I was.' She wore a headband, a skirted running outfit, running shoes and a necklace with a cross. She was asked by an official to leave. She did not.

'I'm a girl, I have a skirt, my hair is done, I have lipstick on and I'm going to run.'

And run she did. While the AAU had no intention of supporting her, the crowd on the day — and other male runners — did. 'The first guy I passed said, 'Go get 'em, girl,'' she recalled. She completed the race with a faster time than ten men — or that is what the records would show if her result had been counted.

But the real result was what Chase-Brand achieved for women's running. She made a deal with the AAU: they would allow longer races for women and she in turn would not make a habit of crashing male races unsanctioned. It was a landmark moment for American female distance runners, and for women who wouldn't be told.

'Julia was like the Grace Kelly of running,' said Amby Burfoot, a long-time editor at *Runner's World* magazine who won the Manchester Road Race nine times, as well as the 1968 Boston Marathon. 'She represented the best of what women's running was to become in the decades that followed — a triumph of ability and determination and a refusal to succumb to barriers.'

Roberta 'Bobbi' Gibb

'I thought about how many preconceived prejudices would crumble when I trotted right along for 26 miles.'

The deal she made with the AAU meant that Julia Chase-Brand never fulfilled her dream of running the Boston Marathon. It was Roberta Gibb who was a direct beneficiary of her actions and made history by being the first woman to run it. Though when she started training she didn't even know it would be an issue.

'I didn't know the marathon was closed to women,' she said in her booklet 'To Boston with Love'. 'I set about training in nurses' shoes with no instructions, no coach and no books. At first, I had no intention of making any kind of statement, I was following my heart for no other reason than I felt moved by some inner force — passion.'

When Gibb started her training there was

no women's movement. It was 1964, Kennedy had just been assassinated and the civil rights movement was still finding its feet. She simply got her boyfriend to pop her on the back of his motorbike, take her further and further distances and then leave her to run back home. Gradually her mileage increased. The next year she took her VW camper van and her puppy, Moot, across California.

Every day I ran for hours and miles in a new place — the hills of Massachusetts, the grassy fields of the Midwest, the open prairies of Nebraska, the Rocky Mountains, the Sierra Nevadas, the coast of California. I'd never seen this earth before, and to me it was wondrous.

I was getting very strong. I could run 40 miles at a stretch. I'd see the top of a distant mountain, small and pale blue in the distance, and I'd spend all day running there, just to stand on the top. Then I'd turn around and run back.

In early 1966 she completed her application to the Boston Athletic Association, only to receive a letter from Will Cloney, the race director, informing her that women were not physiologically capable of running twenty-six miles and furthermore, under the rules that governed international sports, they were not allowed to run.

Bobbi's response? 'All the more reason to run.'

She realised that her running was no longer a personal challenge or an opportunity to see her country. 'I was running to change the way people think . . . If women could do this that was thought impossible, what else could women do? What else can people do that is thought impossible?'

But she was trapped in a Catch-22 situation: how to prove that something was possible if she was not allowed to do it? The answer involved determination, a hoodie and some bushes. Bobbi headed home to Winchester the day before the race. She had a 'huge' roast beef dinner and an apple pie and was then driven by her mum to the start line, wearing a blue sweatshirt with the hood pulled up and her brother's Bermuda shorts, held up with string. She did a couple of miles of warm-up then hid in some bushes near to the start line, afraid that police might arrest her or officials throw her out if they discovered a woman in the runners' midst.

The disguise did not last for long though — male runners behind her soon spotted her feminine figure. But instead of jeers or insults they were supportive. 'They said, 'It's a free road. We won't let anyone throw you out,'' reports Gibb. Encouraged by this response she took off the heavy sweatshirt and let everyone else, runners, crowds and officials, see that she was a woman. A cheer went up and as the race went on the support only increased. As she passed Wellesley College women had heard she was coming and were there waiting, watching for her, crying and screaming. 'One woman standing near, with several children, yelled, 'Ave Maria.' She was crying. I felt as though I was setting them free. Tears pressed behind my own eyes.'

Bobbi, determined not to set women's running back by putting in a bad time, continued to run at pace and eventually came in at 3 hours and 21 minutes, ahead of two-thirds of the male competitors. She was greeted by the Governor of Massachusetts and a roar of applause from spectators and the now-waiting media. The next day it was headline news that a woman had run the Boston Marathon. As Gibb says, 'It changed the way men thought about women, and it changed the way women thought about themselves.'

There was only one small detail — Gibb had been running without a number. She had not been officially allowed to enter so her time was not officially recorded. She had done the women's running community a huge service by showing the world that a woman could complete a marathon, and in under three and a half hours at that. Along the way she had also proved that there was a huge groundswell of support from the men in the running community. But the record books did not take note of her achievement, no matter how many newspapers did.

Bobbi continued to run though — and continued to do it without a number.

I was not running to launch a career or to get publicity for myself. Nor was I running for money. I was running because that's what I loved to do, and I was running to set women free and to over-turn the false beliefs that kept half the world's population in bondage. I wanted to demonstrate in a dignified, competent way that a woman could run the 26-mile distance. Once people understood that, I felt sure the race would open up.

And open up it did, but not yet.

Kathrine Switzer

'*Running made me feel free and powerful. It was what I wanted to do, so I did it.*'

Kathrine Switzer was another of the generation of female distance runners who were not going to let the rules get in the way of their determination to participate in the races they wanted to. As a child she longed to be a cheerleader, until her dude-like father pointed out that it was far better to be the action than to cheer it from the sidelines. So she started to take sport seriously, developing a passion for running as a teenager. At Lynchburg College in Virginia she was encouraged to take part in formal races by the coach there. She ran her first mile race in front of a barrage of astonished local media and went on to receive hate mail as a result. God would, apparently, strike her dead as a result of daring to run with men. 'I was being judged not on my athletic ability but on being a woman,' she says in her memoir *Marathon Woman*.

But Switzer was one of those women who decided that the hatred she received could be converted to inspiration and chose to ignore it. Her dear coach Arnie continued to inspire her with stories of the heroes of the Boston Marathon and her dreams continued to get bigger. One night in 1967 (they trained at night, when they had time) she simply said to him, 'Let's stop talking about Boston and just go and run the damn thing.' The response was not one she was expecting. Instead of supporting her, Arnie was appalled. He told her that women were not capable of running such a distance. Switzer begged to differ, citing the example of Bobbi Gibb and her leap from the bushes as proof. But still Arnie did not want to entertain the idea. He was enraged.

His attitude softened over time (and no doubt with a little cajoling from the formidable Kathrine) and soon the two of them were staring at the race entry form. Kathrine had decided she would run officially or not at all, so they scoured the rule book, only to discover that the sections were divided into 'Men's Track and Field Events', 'Women's Track and Field Events' and then a third category: 'The Marathon', which listed nothing about gender. It seemed that although it was assumed that women were forbidden from running the race, it had not actually been expressly stated anywhere. Will Cloney, on writing to Roberta Gibb those years before, had clearly not done his homework.

Kathrine filled out the requisite paperwork and signed her name: K. V. Switzer, a childhood affectation inspired by writers J. D. Salinger and e. e. cummings. 'Ever since I was twelve I signed all my papers K. V. Switzer, thinking I was totally cool.'

She got on with her training and prepared herself for the big day. She had done a 50km run in preparation, so she knew there was no doubt that she could make the distance. But nerves still kicked in at the thought of blisters, cramps or simply unkind weather. She was right to have worried about the weather — it was a vile combination of snow, sleet and icy winds — but that was not going to be the biggest of her considerable obstacles. As the race began Switzer had to lift her sweatshirt to show the race number on her vest, and as she did so Will Cloney himself herded her through the starting gate, without even noticing that she was a dreaded woman. She had made no attempt to hide her identity, but the bulky clothes and terrible conditions had done it for her.

The race began in earnest and Kathrine felt great. 'At the start of a marathon you are so relieved. You have done all these months of training, it's like going to Mecca. At last, you're the pilgrim, you're making your voyage, so I felt wonderful.' The men around her started to notice that she was female and — as with Bobbi Gibb — instead of reprimanding or reporting her they cheered and congratulated her. She was running alongside her coach Arnie, her boyfriend Tom — a fellow athlete and hammer thrower

— and John Leonard from the college's cross country team. As Kathrine warmed up she discarded her sweatshirt and it was no longer possible to mistake the fact that she was a woman. 'My hair was flying, I didn't try to disguise my gender at all. Heck, I was so proud of myself that I was wearing lipstick!'

Consequently journalists in the press truck took note and started to take pictures. But they didn't stop there; they also started to heckle Cloney's race co-director Jock Semple, a man already known for his temper. Semple, seething at the indignity of his race being 'infiltrated', leaped from the race truck and grabbed Switzer, screaming, 'Get the hell out of my race and give me that race number.' Classy. Switzer was understandably scared to death and tried to dodge him, but he had her by the shirt and was trying to grab her race number.

'He was out of control. It was like being in a bad dream,' she recalls.

Tom, less afraid of a man Semple's size, body-blocked the race director and he 'went flying through the air'. In the stunned pause that followed, Arnie told Kathrine to run like hell, and run she did. Although of course her time was not officially recorded, she finished in 4 hours and 20 minutes. The experience rallied others and made Switzer all the more ballsy about fighting for women to compete in distance running. On return to Syracuse she set up the Syracuse Track Club and encouraged women to join, determined to give women the space to compete.

In 1972 the Boston Marathon relented and women were allowed to compete officially. Switzer continued to work with female runners, in association with cosmetics brand Avon. 'After my experience in Boston, I realized there are plenty of women in the world who grow up without the support I had and without realizing the sky is their only limit. I wanted to reach those women and do something to change their lives. All you need is the courage to believe in yourself and put one foot in front of the other.'

Joan Benoit Samuelson

'When I first started running, I was so embarrassed I'd walk when cars passed me. I'd pretend I was looking at the flowers.

Growing up in Maine during the late 1950s and early 1960s, 'girls just didn't run in public,' Joan Benoit Samuelson has said of her early days as a runner. She took the sport up only as a form of rehabilitation following a

240

skiing accident and found herself excelling pretty quickly. Now that the Boston Marathon, deemed the ultimate marathon on account of it being the world's oldest and having very strict entry qualifications — and one that she first ran and won in 1979 — was open to women, she found herself looking for a greater challenge. She set her heart on the Olympics. Unfortunately the International Olympic Committee had different ideas, because at that time the marathon was still not deemed a suitable Olympic sport for women. It was after all still a time when women had to deal with men who felt threatened by their potential. As Samuelson recounts in a famous TV ad, 'There was a guy who tried to spit on me and push me out of his way.'

By 1984, and with considerable help from a campaign by her sponsors Nike, fighting on her behalf, the inaugural women's Olympic marathon was set to take place. Then, only seventeen days before the Olympic trials, she suffered a knee injury and had to have major surgery. To everyone's surprise, and in a triumph of mental fortitude, she still managed to show up at the trials and win. Three months later she ran — and won — the race itself, in one of the most moving marathon finales of all time. She ran alone for a significant part of the last few miles and entered the famous Los Angeles stadium to huge cheers, having not only done the run of her life, but opened yet further doors to generations of female runners.

Her race wasn't just for the runners of the future though. 'I cried like a baby,' said Julia Chase-Brand of the historic day. 'She gave a tribute to all the women who made distance running possible. I took it as a very personal thank-you. Maybe she was me if I had been born 10 years later.'

Benoit Samuelson continues to be an ambassador for women's running, most notably in her work with Nike where she takes part in the Nike Women's Marathon every year.

13

Injury and You

'Listen to your body. Do not be a blind and deaf tenant.'

Dr George Sheehan

Those who don't have the guts to admit that they don't fancy running often enjoy telling runners about the damage they're doing to their bodies.

Those who have a loved one who runs often worry about them being safe and well.

Those who run often let their imaginations run away with them when in pain — or ignore it entirely.

In each of these instances panic, rumour and a sort of school-girlish Chinese whispers can create horrific anxieties about what is actually going on in a runner's body when they are in pain. Sometimes you just want to be reassured that you are not being neurotic for seeking help about a physical sensation that is entirely natural. Sometimes you need to be told that you're not being idiotic in ignoring a potentially dangerous problem. It

243

is very difficult to tell what is a niggle or natural development in your body, and what is a real issue. Crippling pain can just as often be the result of panic, or simply needing a stretch, as it can be a lasting injury.

I interviewed Anna Barnsley, a physiotherapist who has worked with runners and professional rugby players and accompanied Take That on their last international tour. She has also taught other physios and continues to run her own practice, while following all of the latest research in her field. We did our best to get to the bottom of the top ten running myths that are out there. She is not only a hugely experienced physiotherapist and a fascinating coffee date, but also a very patient woman who remained unfazed by me turning up with a scrappy list of questions and a medical vocabulary that wouldn't put a six-year-old to shame.

The single most important thing she taught me is that pain and your state of mind are intricately linked: pain does not come from your tissues but from your brain. Of course this does not mean that pain does not actually exist, because of course we have all felt it, but it is important to remember that it is produced in the mind. Anna explained that it's the brain's decision to create pain each and every time that something 'painful' occurs, and that decision is based on perceived threat. That threat can be compounded by all sorts of other stresses, creating the vicious cycle of leaving the house for a run in terror of feeling pain and thereby creating pain.

The Truth Behind the Top Ten Running Myths

1) Running will destroy your knees
   'I don't run because I want to be able to bend over when I'm eighty.'

   Every runner has been told this by some smug twerp in the pub who just doesn't have the balls to admit they prefer watching the E! channel or playing *Grand Theft Auto*. These are both admirable pursuits but don't pretend you chose them because of knee pain.

   It seems that much of the bad reputation running has where knees are concerned comes from professional footballers, who are incredibly expensive and highly insured athletes. They are often injected with all sorts of analgesics and encouraged to ignore potential problems so that they can get to the end of a game or tournament without letting anyone down. Then only when they retire (in their late thirties or early forties) do they really see the damage that has been done to them.

Each and every one of us will get wear and tear on our knees whatever we do in life. Some people will get more than others because of their individual biomechanics, and some because of their lifestyles. We're all made differently, but we also all use ourselves differently. Injuries will very rarely be on account of one or the other, but will almost always be a combination of what we're born with and what we do with that. There will always be exceptions to this rule and those with serious injuries that rule out running. But running is not simply a 'hobby that ruins knees'. In fact it's often one that alerts us to more serious problems with our biomechanics and gives us the chance to deal with them before we're hobbling for good. For example, if I had never run I would never have known about the problems I was carrying around in my pelvis and I would certainly have come a cropper later in life. I still dread to think what my pain level would have been had I got

pregnant before this problem was rec-
tified and had something heavy to
carry around in a pelvis which was in
the wrong place. For the sensible recreational runner there should be no
significant problems. For a further look
at knees see the section on iliotibial
band pain on page 258.

2) The high impact of running will give
you a saggy face and a saggy arse
I have had someone who runs a
well-respected beauty salon ask me to
find out if this is the case as so many
of her customers say they won't run
because they dread getting a saggy
face. Women regularly tell me with
great confidence statistics about how
running creates 'twelve times normal
gravity' on your face as though the
skin's very elasticity is bouncing around
like a pair of unsupported boobs. I
don't know how this could possibly
be measured or what it even means
and nor did any doctor or expert I
asked.

What I do now know is that there
is a level of what is called 'oxidative
stress' that is created through exercise. Oxidative stress is the production

of free radicals in the body as a result of exercise, which can cause some damage to the skin's elastic fibres. But all of the other advantages that running provides — improving circulation, getting fresh air, reducing stress — give you a boosted defence against free radicals which will easily counteract that. The argument that oxidative stress ages runners is usually made by the kind of woman who tells you sternly that you should only eat organic chicken as anything else is so full of chemicals, while she has a lit cigarette in her hand.

The single greatest threat to any runner's face or skin will always be sun damage: sunscreen is the answer, not giving up running.

As for the saggy arse — it's bullshit. Running, especially up hills, is pretty much the best thing you can do to have a great bum. Even more so if you're supporting your training with some squats. People who tell you otherwise need to stop talking out of theirs.

3) Running will make you manly looking

The debate about what is or isn't 'ladylike' or 'manly looking' is already an emotive and subjective one. What one of us finds deliciously toned another finds threateningly strong, and where some see femininity others see weakness.

But assuming that the people who suggest this mean 'very muscly' when they say 'manly', you can rest assured that there is nothing specific to running that does this to you. Running is largely an endurance sport, which will build up your slow twitch (or white) muscle fibres. Our muscles are all composed of both slow and fast twitch muscle fibres: the former are what allow our muscles to take on energy while on the move and convert it to motion, while the fast twitch (or red) fibres are what allow us to store power when we are at rest and put it into action in an instant.

Slow twitch muscle fibres do not enlarge the muscles: they are not visible, as can be seen from the physique of a Paula Radcliffe or a Mo Farah. Fast twitch muscle fibres do visibly enlarge the muscles, which is why a sprinter like Usain Bolt looks so much bulkier than a middle- or long-distance runner.

Genetically sprinters will tend to be born with a larger number of fast twitch muscle fibres, which is why they will naturally incline towards that discipline, likewise long-distance runners in reverse.

Ideally a recreational runner wants to work on both groups, so that all of the muscles fibres are working nicely. Running up and down hills as well as interval training is essential to preparing for a marathon as much as completing the long runs. Interval training is the practice of running repeated intervals much faster than usual, with gaps for recovery in between. It is essential for improving cardiovascular fitness and breaking up the repetition of the long runs. 'Fartlek', which means 'speed play' in Swedish, is interval training's more relaxed sibling, and involves running fast bursts within the same run, rather than the more formal stop-start form of intervals. They will give you the instant power to accelerate through a low patch.

Either way, taking up running won't turn you into Rocky. And even if it did, that would be your choice.

4) Running will inflict saggy boobs
As discussed in the chapter on sports bras, running can indeed stretch the ligaments supporting your boobs — especially if you've got larger ones.

A bit of jiggling is OK and entirely normal as the alternative, a horribly restrictive, too small bra, could affect your breathing, but the swinging figure-of-eight motion that a truly unharnessed pair of knockers can make is not ideal.

The solution is simple though: if your boobs can't move around too much when you're running they can't get stretched too much. There are amazing sports bras out there. Get involved.

5) Running makes your knees sound and feel like crisp packets
It is a common sensation to hear or feel a slightly unnerving crunchy or clicking noise in the knees on squatting or rising from a squat. This is called 'crepitus'. Despite sounding

alarmingly close to 'decrepit' it is not in fact particularly dangerous. It usually originates from the patella-femoral joint, which is the interface between the kneecap and the trochlear groove of the femur, or thigh bone, which the kneecap glides along when you bend and straighten the knee.

If crepitus occurs without pain — which it does more often than not — then it is absolutely nothing to worry about. It is not something that will get worse over time, nor is it something specific to running.

However, if you are running a lot and it starts to become associated with pain you should get it looked at. It could be your kneecap dragging on your femur, causing a bit of grinding, or it could mean that the cartilage at the back of the kneecap is wearing out. These are conditions that will need to be treated by a professional.

The problem is often a bio-mechanical issue, where the kneecap is being dragged out to the side by structures on the outer thigh (for example the iliotibial band and lateral quadriceps), often enlarged by recent exercise, which in turn causes rubbing which wears at the cartilage.

The noise does say 'Danger!' very loudly in one's brain, making it hard to ignore, but it is not as bad a situation as it can so often sound.

6) The type of cardiovascular exercise that running involves is no good for weight loss
The 'fat-burning' zone that equipment in fancy gyms or swishy personal trainers talk about refers to any period of exercise when your heart is working at 60–70 per cent of its maximum rate. This is probably what you feel like on a slow run, the sort of jog where you might admire the leaves on a tree, or the bottom of someone running ahead of you. This pace does indeed burn more fat than when you are exercising at a more intense rate.

However, a slightly higher heart rate uses up far more calories, which is actually what is most important for weight loss.

So while there is some truth in the suggestion that running does not always work your body within the

253

fat-burning zone this does not mean that it is no good for weight loss. Far from it.

7) Running makes you wee blood
The kind of fuss I would make if I saw blood in my urine doesn't bear thinking about, so the fact that some long-distance runners see it as normal rather frightens me.

Seeing blood in your urine is not normal. You must take notice of it. It is not entirely uncommon in extreme athletes but it is indicative of a problem, not a nice blast of hard work.

If someone pees blood after a long run they need a glass of water and a doctor's appointment to check out their kidneys at the very least. It is not entirely known why blood is some-times seen in urine after extreme exercise — the current thinking is that it might be to do with the way red blood cells break away during exercise — but in an average runner it is more likely to indicate kidney problems, dehydration or overuse of painkillers, which are so often harsh on the stomach and kidneys.

Running does not do this to you as a matter of course and it should never be ignored.

8) Running makes your wee smell of ammonia

Running — or any extreme exercise — can make your wee smell of ammonia. But it shouldn't. If you get a whiff of that distinctive smell when you go to the bathroom it means that you are carbohydrate deficient and need to look at your diet. The smell is caused by the breakdown of muscle protein and is a result of running without enough of the right kind of fuel.

The brain needs glucose to function and it cannot get glucose from fat, only from carbohydrates. While you may be a runner with body fat — you may even be a bit overweight and on a diet — the brain and body cannot access that glucose from your fat stores. Consequently if you are attempting exercise without enough fuel the body will start to break down proteins to access glucose. It is the amino acids in those proteins breaking down that causes the smell.

9) Running will cause vaginal prolapse
I was shocked when someone asked me in all seriousness if this was the case. And I was even more shocked when physiotherapist Anna Barnsley did not dismiss the suggestion as entirely out of the question, although I am not sure Take That or a rugby team have ever found reason to chat to her about that before. But, mercifully, running alone does not and cannot cause vaginal prolapse in a normal healthy person.

However, if you already have a tendency towards it, and childbirth is its most common cause, the high impact of pounding the pavements can bring it on. 'But surely just a sneeze in the garden centre on a sunny day could do that?' I asked Anna and she grudgingly agreed. She was, however, very firm that running also exercises your pelvic floor muscles, which counteracts the risk of prolapse by strengthening the area.

10) Running will make you die younger by using up your life's energy faster
This is a suggestion that has divided the people I've mentioned it to into

two neat halves: those who nod solemnly and say that yes, it is entirely true and very worrying. And those who think I have finally become untethered from my already tenuous grip on reality for even considering this a proposition worth researching.

It seems that this myth comes from the absurd idea that we each have a finite number of heartbeats in our lives, and by increasing your heart rate through running you will use them up faster. There is so much research to show that life expectancy is extended by not just running but most exercise that this is an entirely absurd suggestion. Honestly it is pure madness. Try to smile pityingly at the people who think it, as they probably still believe in witches.

And then there are actual injuries. Yes, sometimes running does hurt — and not just in the 'oh my, that was a stiff wind this morning, my ears are stinging' sense. Here are the five most common injuries among runners, how to identify them and how best to cope with them.

1) Iliotibial band syndrome
This is the most common source of

pain for regular runners by a significant margin, particularly long-distance runners.

The iliotibial band is a fascia that runs across the upper outside of the thigh from knee to hip. The repetitive action of running can put a large amount of stress on it, causing it to tighten and shorten after runs of more than half an hour or so. This in turn can cause fiery pain in both the outer side of the knees and up in the hips. It starts off as a mild discomfort and ends up causing agony, leaving you in despair of ever running again and tackling staircases tearfully in reverse. It is a genuine torment for many runners, as it's impossible to tell if it has gone until you have been running a while. It tends to make its reappearance when you're tired, possibly being rained on, a few miles from home and feeling rather low. Like a bastard ex-boyfriend who sends you a flirty text every time you think you might be moving on.

While both of these things are common, neither is insurmountable and there is a lot that can be done to alleviate or prevent iliotibial band (or ITB) pain.

In the short term, buying a foam roller (a large, brightly coloured foam rolling-pin-type object that looks not dissimilar to a buoyancy aid or a prop from *Gladiators*) and lying on your side massaging the fascia during *X Factor* is an excellent solution. While initially painful this does a great job of relieving tension in the ITB and can be a huge help with the pain. It does not solve the problem of why you are getting the pain though.

Therefore, in the long term, it is important to work out why the iliotibial band is shortening. There can be many reasons for this. The most common is because the gluteus medius muscle on the outer buttock is not strong enough or not working hard enough. This muscle is the one you can see, the outer muscle lying on top of the others or, as I call it 'the Kardashian muscle'. It is this one that turns the leg outwards. In many of us the leg can be inclined to turn inwards, collapsing the arch and making the foot flatter, which is called 'pronating'. This lack of proper foot control as the foot hits the ground (which many fancy trainers claim to eradicate entirely) lets the knees roll inwards, creating tension on the ITB. This is generally a result of an insufficient gluteus medius and can be helped enormously by activating and strengthening the muscle.

You can of course investigate further, asking why your gluteus medius isn't strong enough in the first place. At some point the answer will relate to the fact that instead of spending our days clambering over fields picking berries and chasing animals for dinner, we spend hours of each day watching telly and wanging around on the Internet. Bits of our bodies are unused like never before, so when we suddenly challenge them our muscles are quite reasonably a little startled — if not ultimately relieved.

While there are a lot of exercises you can look up online as well as hundreds of 'helpful' YouTube videos, which I suspect are more often watched by curious 14-year-old boys with a developing taste for physiotherapists in Lycra, it is always worth finding a professional who can look at exactly which muscles need to be reactivated and how. I am of the opinion that investing in a decent physiotherapist and spending an hour working out some specifics with them is a far better use of time and effort than trying on numerous pairs of trainers and bleating to your loved ones about how your new hobby hurts. Doing a few (admittedly very boring) exercises can generally do a much better job of solving the problem than spending hundreds of pounds on the right corrective running shoe or orthotic insert. Save it for getting someone attractive to talk to you reassuringly while rubbing your thighs, and then buy a running top you feel a bit sexier in. Everyone's happier this way.

2) Plantar Fasciitis
Plantar fasciitis sounds like a baddie from a science-fiction novel, but is in fact a very sore foot. It is pain in the heel and sole of the foot that creates a very realistic sensation of either running barefoot on hot coals or of having worn through your heel altogether.

As with ITB pain, plantar fasciitis

is most common when a runner is at the peak of their training and taking on longer and harder runs than they have ever done before. This is also when they can least cope with a painful and confusing injury. And as with ITB pain it is caused by tightness in the body's fascia, in this instance in the foot area. The fascia is a tissue that each of us has covering our entire body. While I sat, gagging and squealing over my cappuccino like a first-time passenger on a roller-coaster, Anna explained to me that the best way to imagine the fascia is like that film which you see when you pull the skin off a raw chicken. That opaque, slimy, cling-film-like connective tissue between the meat and the skin. For years I thought that my ITB was red and sinewy like a piece of muscle, but apparently I was living a lie.

The creepiest thing of all is that the fascia is one continuous tissue, enveloping every single tissue, muscle and organ in your body. It wraps around your stomach, intestines, spinal chord, brain. There is no beginning to it and no end, although it is thicker in some places such as along the length of the thighs (the ITB) and under the arch of the foot. I find this simultaneously fascinating and repulsive, as if each of us has a never-ending sci-fi beast within.

Medical science has only recently started learning that the fascia also has some bearing on communication within the body. We already know that the blood and the neural system hold vital roles in transporting both messages and substances around the body, but now it seems the fascia can also communicate. What this means is that if you have tension in one part of your body it will often create tension somewhere else, hence the idea of 'referred pain' and the popularity of reflexology.

Over-stretching can cause inflammation of the fascia and this is what is behind plantar fasciitis. Typically it will occur in someone who has a pronating foot action as they will tend to repeatedly over-stretch the fascia when the foot rolls over.

People mistakenly believe that yet more stretching will ease the pain.

This will not help and will only exacerbate the problem, particularly if it is only in the early stages of the condition. In the short term the best way to alleviate the pain is to get a bottle of water and pop it in the freezer, then to use the frozen bottle to roll up and down the length of the foot like a rolling pin. That, and rest, will ease both the inflammation and pain. This is an injury that responds well to rest, but in the long term it is worth looking at your running style and the condition of the supporting muscles to the area.

3) Achilles Tendonopathy
This used to be referred to — and sometimes still is in older reference books and darker recesses of the Internet — as Achilles tendonitis because it was believed until relatively recently that the condition was a result of inflammation. (Apparently the suffix '-itis' denotes inflammation.)

However, it has recently been discovered that it is actually a physiological change in the tendon fibres at the back of the ankle, caused by repetitive overload on the area.

When the Achilles tendon is over-loaded (the diplomatic medical term for 'over-trained' or 'overused') the body recognises that it is under increased stress and starts to change its fibre composition. Over time a tendon that once had the springy qualities of a fresh stick of celery takes on the fibrous stiffness of a root of ginger. Not so malleable and significantly stiffer. This in turn causes that stiffness and pain that many runners will be familiar with.

If you were to look at the tendons under a microscope at this point you'd be able to see that there are actually more cells, or a bigger 'cellular matrix'. This is caused by more blood vessels feeding into it to try and make the tendon tough enough to cope with the overload. The problem is that this becomes counterproductive because to carry on running you want a nice boingy tendon.

No matter how diplomatic the use of the term 'overload' is, Achilles tendonopathy is an injury caused by overwork. If the biomechanics of your body or the way that you run means that you put a lot of stress on that area, the most effective thing you can do is to rest. Think of it as an excuse to catch up on some boxsets with your feet up. Running 'through' the injury won't help, even if getting the blood flowing through the area makes it feel better in the short term.

4) Piriformis Syndrome
The piriformis is a tiny muscle that sits between the other gluteal muscles in the buttocks. One of the problems with this muscle is that it sits right over the sciatic nerve, so that when someone is diagnosed as having sciatica or back pain they are sometimes in fact suffering from an overactive piriformis muscle. This feels as if someone has just jabbed a red-hot knitting needle into your bum from the side, as if they were planning to barbecue both your buttocks as a sort of human kebab. It is also a very hard location to describe when it is causing you pain. You're often reduced to pointing at your own arse and gasping, 'So . . . sore! In . . . there!'
There are just so many surrounding muscles, tendons and nerves that it seems impossible to articulate what

you're actually feeling. The greatest immediate relief you can get is from finding an old tennis ball (spiky built-for-purpose rubber balls are also available in sports shops) and sitting on it, rolling your buttocks around until you hit the spot. In the long term this is an injury usually caused by some kind of problem within the pelvis. As with iliotibial band pain, relieving the condition long enough to get through an event and working out the cause are two very different things. It's up to you how far you want to take it.

5) Ankle Sprain

There is little that can be done to avoid this one, beyond looking where you're going. It's easily done and incredibly common, especially if you're not concentrating. An ankle sprain is simply the result of placing your foot incorrectly and turning it over as you wobble off a pavement or out of a car, or by misjudging a piece of craggy ground if running in the countryside. The sprain itself refers to rolling the foot inwards so that the underside of the foot turns in and the structures on the outer part of the ankle are massively over-stretched.

I am particularly proud of having done this from a sitting position by getting up to go to the bathroom without first realising that my foot had gone numb. I took two steps on a waggling misplaced foot before the pain hit me and I spent two weeks on crutches. Not strictly a running injury, but one that means I know this REALLY HURTS. Rest, ice, compression and elevation are your friends here (these are what the RICE leaflets in doctors' waiting rooms refer to).

6) A Stitch
Yes, I appreciate that I told you it was the top five injuries and a stitch isn't strictly an injury, but I am not sure there is any pain worse than having a stitch. It somehow paralyses you with an evil pincer movement of pain and shame. Why does getting a stitch make you feel so idiotic? Surely you should just have had some water or stretched properly, or done whatever it is that you're supposed to do to avoid getting one? Why does something so simple, so childlike, feel so utterly debilitating?

A small consolation is that no one really knows what it is that you are meant to do to get over or avoid a stitch — it turns out that there are all sorts of theories still being expounded about what they are. Currently the received wisdom is that it's a spasm of the diaphragm. The diaphragm is a muscle so using it irregularly, or creating irregular breathing patterns by becoming out of breath at either the start or a difficult part of a run, will make it contract out of sync and cause pain.

The best thing you can do is to try and breathe through it, to regulate your breathing by really getting your ribcage to expand and contract. Beyond that we're still waiting for the scientists' next big theory.

14

Getting Your Kicks

'You have brains in your head. You have feet in your shoes. You can steer yourself in any direction you choose. You're on your own, and you know what you know. And you are the guy who'll decide where to go.'

Dr. Seuss

Trainers are pretty much all you really need to start running, and there are even those who would argue that you don't need them at all. You can certainly get away with 'these things I used to wear in the gym five years ago' for a good few weeks. But if you're either running with a view to a specific event or you've decided that you're going to really go for it for a few months, a decent pair of something squishy and supportive on your feet will save a fair amount of pain in the long run. The problem is that you have to buy them. And buying your first pair of trainers can be more painful than even the harshest marathon.

Entering a sportswear shop alone for the first time can be overwhelming. Attempting to buy my first pair of trainers was one of the most terrifying, humiliating and dispiriting experiences of my life, and I've interviewed Naomi Campbell.

All you are trying to do is find something that will take just a milligram of the pain away from those first runs, but it can feel like an assessment of the most committed and intrusive kind. It should not be as hard as it often feels — after all it's just buying some rubber and canvas to cover your feet. Since that first proper purchase before my first London Marathon I've done this many times and in many different environments.

Top Ten Tips for Buying Trainers Without Having to Exchange Them for Your Dignity

1) Don't leave the shop with a pair of trainers that you find aesthetically distressing

    Running shoes are never going to be exquisite, but their strange stripes, swooshes and signs can be peculiarly pleasing. Before I ran I always found tennis shoes to have the most charm and had to be talked out of buying

271

them on more than one occasion by those more knowledgeable than me. These days I still care what my trainers look like but I am prepared to compromise on looks for something that isn't going to be actively doing me harm. Nevertheless I remain convinced that the single most important thing about trainers is that you're not repulsed by putting them on: if you don't want to wear them, you probably won't, and if you're not wearing them you're not going to run.

2) Don't go trainer shopping in a short skirt and no tights Should you be actively seeking the attention of an eager chap in shiny tracksuit bottoms this is the ideal outfit: he'll be kneeling at your ankles for most of the process. If you just want to find something to go running in perhaps wear something that'll make you feel a little less self-conscious while he's down there.

3) Allow yourself enough time
It sounds so obvious, but as with the most dreaded tasks they often end up

happening as a result of a sudden burst of 'I'll just get it over and done with'. But the staff who'll be measuring you up often like to faff. They want to do their job properly and this involves a lot of chat. Just go with it. Don't give yourself ten minutes then succumb to the small trickle of sweat wending its way down your spine as you panic about whether you're standing right and how late you are going to be for lunch.

4) Set a budget before you go in
Trainers come in a huge variety of prices. There is no need to spend £100 on your first pair just to reassure yourself your feet are not going to turn black and drop off. If you want fancy trainers, go nuts — there are plenty around. But they won't make a big enough difference if you're just planning to get to the park and back for a few weeks. Summon the same courage required for walking through a department-store beauty hall while non-specifically aged women with tangerine skin waft scent at you and talk lustfully of promotions. £50 is a

reasonable expectation. You can pay less if you are smart about finding old models online, and of course there is a lot out there for more.

5) Know what to expect
There are three main techniques that running shops use to measure what type of shoe you'll need. They will either film you running on a treadmill, then look at the footage of what your feet and ankles are doing; ask you to run across a heat sensitive pad that will show how your feet are landing when you hit the pad; or simply ask you to run up and down the street outside the shop while they watch. Clearly option three is not ideal. Especially if you are new to running. Running twenty metres in front of a shop assistant you've never met feels as natural as having a quick baby while you're asking where the cotton wool is in a pharmacy. Increasingly shops have more sophisticated ways of looking at your gait and they are usually in fairly discreet areas of the shop. Nike Town and Sweatshop are particularly well-designed stores which bear discretion in mind.

6) Understand what the diagnosis is

What the sales person is looking to understand is which part of your foot hits the ground first as you run, how it hits the ground and how one of their shoes can help to keep this balanced. The most common 'flaw' is the previously mentioned but hugely bothersome pronating, which is when your feet roll in slightly as you hit the ground. There are trainers that can offer support in your instep for this so that your knees and hips are not taking the hit every time you step out. Some retailers call this 'over-pronating', some merely 'pronating'. Some runners will 'under-pronate', which is less common and sees your feet rolling slightly outwards. If you do neither you will be described as a 'neutral runner'.

7) Remember that you are a work in progress

This is hugely important. It is easy to cling to your diagnosis, happily having medicalised your 'problem', and to leave the shop with the most expensive remedial trainers. But pronating doesn't need to be a permanent condition. Often it's nothing to do with the structure of your feet, but simply a result of having a weak bum and thighs which are just letting your legs flop in a bit. After all you're not yet a runner. Don't let yourself be bamboozled by this. If the sales assistant winces and points at the most high-spec shoes in the shop, simply thank them for their time and spend the extra cash on an appointment with a physio. Then go back to the shop when you *really* know how badly you pronate.

8) Know your pronating from your prolapsing
When my sister decided to reignite her running self after her baby was born I took her to Nike Town to buy her trainers as a birthday present. I sat unobtrusively, filled with a sisterly sense of respect and goodwill for her post-baby weight-loss mission, until I felt I really needed to step in. That point came when I heard her confidently telling the assistant that she definitely didn't pronate when she had her baby. It was all fine, apparently.

9) Leave your issues with the colour pink at the door

Pink is a pretty colour. I am as devoted to my hot pink Nars Schiap lipstick as I am to my Myla rose pink negligee. But pink skipping ropes and pink boxing gloves especially designed for 'lady exercise' make me flush with an altogether more ragey pink. Yet where trainers are concerned you can drive yourself mad if you try to avoid any at all. It's just a colour.

10) Try to remember it's for fun. You're doing it for you.

15

Get Involved

'Years ago, women sat in kitchens drinking coffee and discussing life. Today, they cover the same topics while they run.'
Joan Benoit Samuelson

As research has consistently shown, while health is the leading motivator in getting people to run it is never the thing that will keep them running. It's the social side of running that does that. Whether your running becomes social or improves your social life outside of running, that is what will keep you — literally — on track. For many, joining a running club is the only way to do this. But for many others the very thought of a running club is enough to bring on a sharper attack of breathlessness than sprint training ever could. Like finding the right hairdresser or the right husband you often have to try a few first to find out what sort of person you are and what you are prepared to put up with. Some are all about chasing time and competing against other clubs;

others are about wider social movements, making running almost secondary. These running clubs err rather more on the heartfelt than the heart rate.

Parkrun

Taking place up and down the country at 9 a.m. on Saturday mornings parkrun is a totally free, locally organised 5k run that absolutely anyone can turn up to and take part in, on the condition that they volunteer at events once or twice a year as well. It is without doubt the most inclusive, friendly environment I have ever run in, and one that helped me become a greater part of my community as both a runner and a volunteer steward. Standing in my high-vis jacket and three jumpers as a steward for a January parkrun I watched the neon murmuration of amateur runners take off up Hove park with a tear in my eye that was not a mere result of the wind chill. Every single runner is clapped in, whether it takes them sixteen minutes or sixty. Families come and watch their loved ones, dogs scamper around and everyone hangs out afterwards. It is a joy and there will be one near you.

Nike Run Club/Sweatshop Running Community/Sweaty Betty Running Club

These are just three of the better-known examples, but most running stores now arrange weekly (or more frequent) runs for those who wish to turn up. They are usually free, with proper guides and an elected runner at the back of the pack to make sure that no one is left behind. They are a brilliant starting point and a surprisingly soft touch regarding the shops themselves. I had feared relentless salesmanship, but found only runners who wanted to find other runners.

GoodGym

Based in East London but with offshoots around the country coming soon, GoodGym is a running club that keeps the running side of things somewhat on the back-burner. Once or twice a week the group meets then runs across town to do a good deed, whether it is helping to clear soil from a community garden, helping a pensioner with limited mobility to fix a wall or converting derelict land in urban areas. The elderly that are visited are encouraged to share their wisdom. Then the group runs back.

Run Dem Crew

The brainchild of Charlie Dark, a DJ, poet and teacher, Run Dem Crew are most definitely Not A Running Club. Dark describes them as 'a racing crew that actively encourages all members to enter races and represent the shirt'. Terrifying though that sounds they are not an elite bunch and encourage all abilities, stating that 'it's not how fast you go but how you cross the finish line'. They also have an RDC Youngers project with a strong emphasis on mentoring, which other members are encouraged to contribute to. With branches in East and West London they are breathtakingly stylish and have hearts of gold.

Digital Running Clubs

As the apps available become ever more sophisticated and the popularity of social networking continues to grow, the support and encouragement that you can get online is extraordinary. You can keep in touch, mark your progress and meet at national races. Welcome to the future!

16

The Perfect Running Style

'I'm a greater believer in luck, and I find the harder I work the more I have of it.'
Thomas Jefferson

There are entire books written about how to achieve the perfect running style, but there is no perfect running style. There is a technical ideal, but those who have broken records or inspired millions are rarely the ones using it. The search for the perfect gait remains something almost as contentious as the barefoot running debate, in which various factions of runners argue that it is better and 'more natural' to run without shoes while others remain loyal to every technological advance that the industry can dream up. It is impossible to dictate what is best for everyone as our individual biomechanics are so different. I would no more presume to dictate how we all run than to prescribe one specific dance style for womankind.

The single most important thing to remember is that we can all run. It's an instinct we had as children, and despite adult lives in front of the computer or telly eating carbs we are still able to increase our stride in case of emergency. There is no 'I can't run'. If you have legs and lungs you can run.

However, those years sitting curled up on sofas or wedged into unsatisfactory train seats, as well as our own personalities and attendant neuroses, will have an effect on how we run when we go beyond fifty metres. To try and straighten these out from day one, or at least to give you the confidence that you're not doing yourself actual harm, there are some basic guidelines you can follow.

Running Rules for Everyone

Aim for a mid-foot strike

When I began running I tried very, very hard to do two things in order to show as much willing as possible: to bounce up and down as springily as possible, and to reach out as far as possible as I could with my heels. I interpreted both of these actions as indicators of serious commitment to my sport and a huge signifier of great athleticism. I could not have been more wrong.

The ideal part of your foot to land on is not your heel. This is a myth perpetuated by both cartoon runners who spring into action with their foot fully flexed and the huge aerated trainers of the 1980s and 1990s. Barefoot runners believe that those big squashy trainers are responsible for making us all run incorrectly, and that we should be aiming for our toes. In the absence of any conclusive research proving them correct, or indeed correct for modern, western runners, it seems the truth lies somewhere in between: we should aim to land in the middle of our foot. Not right up on the balls of our toes, but an inch or so lower so we can still give ourselves a bit of leverage as we leave the ground, without having to roll over our entire foot from heel to toe.

If we were to emulate the perfect running style it would be 1960s cartoon character Penelope Pitstop's. She has a lovely, if extreme, wide stride and lands correctly on her feet, even if she is wearing rather impractical white leather go-go boots.

As for the bounciness I was wrong there as well. It seems obvious now, but it takes as much effort to be trotting along with bouncy short strides as it does to reach out and get a bit Pitstop about things. Aim for the latter, although perhaps not exactly like the latter. We don't after all have Hanna-Barbera to sort us out in case of injury.

Never forget your arms

You need your arms for running more than you think. Try a spin to the end of your street and back with your hands shoved in your pockets and you'll realise just how useful they are. But don't over-think it. When you're running, keep your shoulders down and let the momentum of your arms create propulsion; use your arms' power to drive you along. The best way to imagine them working is to think of the effort going into powering them backwards, so that the swing forwards is both relaxing and propelling. This feels counterintuitive at first, but once it has clicked it seems alarmingly obvious.

'Arms run hills' is one of my dad's favourite nuggets of advice, and reluctant though I was to admit it he is right. This is where the arm swing is reversed as the gradient of the ground beneath you changes and you need to push forwards to help yourself up the hill. It feels as if you are punching the air and makes you thankful for those press-ups you've done.

Don't let yourself get too tense though. Clenched fists with gripped thumbs or arms swinging wildly across your body rather than loosely at your side will not help you. These actions will only transfer tension up to your neck and shoulders and leave you wondering how on earth a sport performed with your legs is making you want a neck massage.

Look after your head

Heads are heavy — don't leave yours lolling around. It sounds daft, but if you spend twenty minutes running with your gaze directed at your toes the weight of your own head is going to be dragging you down and putting a great deal of pressure on your neck. Of course you need to check where you're putting your feet from time to time, but try to keep looking up and forwards so that your spine is straight and you can see a broader landscape.

Visualise yourself being pushed rather than reaching forwards

Again this is something that I was daft about for months. Even once I had got rid of my bizarre heel strike I continued to reach forward with my knees, as if I were dragging my body behind them. Of course you do have to run with your knees reaching forwards, but it feels considerably easier once you imagine yourself being pushed from behind. Focus on your leg kicking up as you leave the ground while your bum and the backs of your thighs are pushing you forwards. This makes the biggest difference when you start to get tired and feel your body sagging. If you visualise a kindly (or perhaps just fanciable) chap giving you a shove from behind, you get a surprisingly large boost.

Do some complementary exercises

No runner should just run, and part of achieving the perfect gait should also be about giving it a break. Should you get into it and be running a few times a week, aiming to run a certain distance or in a certain time, you'll need to start doing a bit of extra work beyond your running to strengthen and support key muscles and to make sure that you don't pick up any bad habits that might cause you pain later down the line.

If you do some simple abdominal, arm and butt exercises you will massively reduce your risk of injury and feel significantly stronger. Pilates is also excellent for this. Go swimming, go for a long walk or just spend an evening in front of *EastEnders* doing some stretching. It all counts.

Relax

If you are terrified of running, your body will recognise this and you will be spilling adrenalin and tension throughout your body. Try to relax and remember that this is something you have chosen to do. Warming up properly will help with this, as well as some key stretches afterwards. You took time out of your day to enjoy it and your body will ultimately thank you for it. Keep your shoulders down and your eyes up. You should be proud of what you're doing: that is the most important thing about any running style.

17

The Big One:
Everything you wanted to know
about a marathon
but were too afraid to ask

*''Man this hurts, I can't take it anymore.'
The hurt part is an avoidable reality, but
whether or not you can stand any more is
up to the runner himself. This pretty
much sums up the most important aspect
of marathon running.'*

Haruki Murakami

For some, running around the neighbourhood will provide more than enough stimulation.
For others, myself included, entering public
events are a necessary motivation. Whether
it's chasing an improved time, the thrill of the
crowd's roar or simply receiving the recogni-
tion of other runners around you from time to
time, they are a valid endeavour whatever
your standard. It doesn't mean they can't
push your nerves to previous unknown levels
of activity though. Regardless of how well you
have prepared your mind and body the tiniest

of practicalities can still trip you up. And even if they don't end up catching you out they can still cause you sleepless nights. Here I offer you the benefit of my past mistakes and successes.

Doing It for Charity

Charity or 'Golden Bond' places for big events — particularly the London Marathon — are the easiest way to take part. Marathons or half marathons in big cities are hugely expensive to stage: logistics include road closures, marshals, liaison with the police and emergency services, and the transportation and security of bags. While these larger races usually have a number of random ballot places the vast majority of spots are turned over to charities to allocate to runners who have applied to them. If you don't want the pressure of fund-raising on your first big race, smaller ones and countryside events are usually inexpensive to take part in, but be warned — what you lose in pressure to fund-raise you also lose in support en route. There is no doubt that I would not have got round my first marathon if not for my obligation to the charity I was running for. Without constantly reminding myself of the lives of those I was helping I would surely have buckled under the weight of what I was attempting.

But how does the system work? Charities buy the number of places for a few hundred pounds each and then give amateur runners the chance to take part — on the condition that they raise significantly more money than the cost of the place itself. Every now and then a newspaper or a documentary will pop up discussing the 'scandal' of how charities are expected to buy these places, rather than every single person involved in manning roads, driving trucks and checking bags doing it for free, but I rarely take much heed. A phenomenal amount of money is created by people taking on a feat that seems beyond them and I struggle to see the problem with that. It is a truly humbling experience to share a race with those less able than you, those injured by war or disease or those running in memory of loved ones lost.

What I do have a problem with is the small number of runners who take on a marathon in response to some existential crisis, commit little to the training over the six-month build-up and then send out a handful of slightly passive-aggressive emails demanding a tenner the week before the big day. I believe that if you are asking people to sponsor you for a long-distance run you have earned the right to ask because it's a huge, daunting challenge that you have taken on. People don't sponsor you for the day you spend in a beautiful major city, being cheered and heralded by strangers as a hero. They sponsor you for the dark, lonely mornings when you get up before the heating has come on just to get that extra 5k done. They sponsor you for the parties you attend without touching a drop of alcohol because you have a long run planned for the next day. They sponsor you as a show of support to your loved ones, who are bored rigid of having you roll around on the floor complaining about your tight hamstrings. They sponsor you because you are paying tribute to the pain that others suffer by undergoing an experience that will at times hurt you.

But during a period when you might already be busier than ever with running (and endless stretching) fund-raising can be an added stress. Here are some tips on how to get on top of the situation:

Choose your charity carefully
Obviously if your running is inspired by a specific person or event this decision will be easier. But make sure you have properly

looked into the charities that are offering places and what they do. It will make all of those wise-ass 'Why should I effectively be funding your hobby?' comments a lot easier to deal with if you know why you have chosen your charity. And it will make the darkest points of the run much more bearable if you can properly visualise the pain that you are easing in others by experiencing your own.

Get a fund-raising page online
www.justgiving.com and www.virginmoney are the two best known and most reliable. They have revolutionised the whole process, indeed they have largely removed the horror of having to write down everyone's offers of cash and then chase them up for cheques indefinitely after the event. They allow you to personalise your site with photos and text, to link to social networks and to keep up to date with who is sponsoring you and when. And you can either send individual thank-yous or one large group one after the event.

Be clear and honest about why you are doing the run
If you simply want to prove to yourself that you can run the distance that you have

chosen, be honest about that. There is little that people will spot faster than some spurious fear of brittle bone disease or a made-up uncle you have never mentioned who is suddenly dying of an obscure illness. These tricks are entirely transparent, insulting to people's intelligence and can do more harm than good. It's far easier to respect someone who simply tells the truth: 'I have wanted to try running this distance for years and as motivation I have researched the charities and chosen to work with this one because of X and Y. I'm hoping this will help me get to the end so do bung me a tenner if you have one going spare.'

Use social media

Don't just use social media forty-eight hours before the event to post a jumbled selection of panicky messages in UPPERCASE LOUD VOICE about how awful it's going to be because you've been so busy, you've hardly trained. No one cares and they certainly won't feel like stumping up their earnings if that's how you approach things.

Post regular updates on how the training is going — keep a diary on Facebook or hashtag posts and pictures on Instagram or Twitter. Let people in on what a struggle it has been on icy January runs, or let them whoop with you when you reach significant milestones. However lonely you might feel at times, no one runs these events alone, and knowing what you've been through is far more likely to inspire people to sponsor what is months' worth of commitment, not just one magical day.

Beware the power of the celebrity 'retweet'

Asking celebrities to post a link to your sponsorship web page on their timeline is of very little use. The vast majority of the time they won't do it anyway, and when they do their Twitter followers will very rarely click on the link. This is particularly acute in the week or so before a big event when Twitter can start to seem like a big, jangly begging bowl being waved in everyone's face. It is significantly more effective — and appropriate — to ask specific people who you have a connection with than to rely on the potential kindness of strangers.

Don't forget the power of the corporate cash pot

Try asking your company for some corporate sponsorship. A lot of smaller companies are happy to stump up a bit of money for you to run with their logo on your outfit, while others are simply happy to contribute to a healthy, worthwhile pursuit for their employees. And if you work for a bigger company it is worth getting them on side so you can send company-wide emails promoting any events you are holding to raise funds.

Be imaginative

You don't have to ask people to sponsor you just for the race day itself. There is a world of other sponsorship ideas that you can dip into, from bake sales at the office to asking people for their unwanted things that you can sell on eBay for funds. Imagination will always be a more effective fund-raising tool than relentless nagging.

Be strategic

Divide up the amount that you need to raise, or the amount that you are aiming to raise, and work out how many people you know who might realistically be able to sponsor you a few pounds. Ask them. And then get creative with the others. Don't repeatedly ask people who won't be able to afford actual money for it — it's rude. It's easier to play to people's strengths, getting help from those with time, and money from those with money.

Be polite

No one is obliged to sponsor you. You have chosen to do this. It is your responsibility. So don't be impatient if people don't immediately cough up. Be as lavish with your thanks as you are with your requests.

Maintain a sense of humour

Running and its attendant needs can be funny, undignified and ridiculous. Being po-faced about threshold runs and lactic acid is not necessary just because you are raising money for a worthy cause. Maintain a sense of humour — you might need it in other people before the end of your running adventure.

Work with others you're running with, not against them

Find out if there are others in your area running for the same charity and if you can work with them on events. More than one set of contacts at an event can make more of a splash and keep spirits high if you end up selling baked goods at a drizzly fete with no one else but the toothless guy from the coconut shy for company.

Don't leave it until the last minute
This really is one of the most important points. As with anything to do with money, avoiding the issue is not going to make it go away. If you feel awkward asking people, updating social media or doing specific emails you are still going to be obliged to get the required money to the charity. The way they see it your social anxieties are less of a problem than those being endured by the people on whose behalf they work.

Put the link to your fund-raising page as your email signature or in the biog of your Twitter or Facebook profile, so you can alert people without having to address it directly at first. But don't ignore the fact that you've got a certain amount to raise. The charities will help you, but they can't do it all. As with the running itself . . . the only way to do it is to, well, do it.

Keep in touch with the charity
Most of the charities who work with running events are very good at keeping their runners

informed regarding where the funds are going and why they are needed. It is a huge motivation to be able to visualise what the money you are raising can actually be turned into. There is usually a specific contact at the charities who can get back to you if you need help or have queries, and they always send a team on the day to cheer you on. Make that connection if you can. Smaller charities in particular are hugely grateful for the funds and the difference they make is immediate and tangible.

Looking Good for Marathon Day

The confidence that running has given me in my appearance is immeasurable. There are people who have seen me in sports kit before or after a run who I would never have let see me entirely without make-up five years ago. But public running events are occasions where there are both professional and amateur photographers in abundance. I want to look good in those pictures. By 'good' I mean strong, powerful and inspiring. And, more than that, knowing that you don't quite look like death, even if you feel like it, is indisputably cheering.

Consequently I have put an inordinate

amount of time and effort into researching what beauty products look good, make me feel good and, crucially, don't disintegrate before I have encountered my first glucose drink. These are my essentials:

Nail polish
Nail polish is the perfect boost for running. I love it anyway, but when I am taking part in a public race I have a positively Brontë-esque passion for having sparkly flashes of colour on my fingernails. I have run in Tom Ford 'Perfect Coral', Chanel 'Peridot' (a greeny gold) and Essie 'Clam Bake'. For the San Francisco Marathon I yearned for a certain sparkly top-coat that a friend ended up travelling across the whole of London for, as she knew how much my marathon nails are part of me. It is almost impossible to chip or ruin nail polish while distance running, which makes it the King of Products for these purposes.

As far as my toes are concerned I prefer to leave them bare, just so I can fully survey any damage incurred when I get home. Make sure you cut and file your toenails about three or four days before the event so that they are neat but not so cropped that they leave flesh beyond the nail. This really hurts after three or four hours of running.

Eyeliner

For my first marathon I knew that I wanted to use one item of make-up that would stand out, would stay the distance and would make me feel like a sort of disco goddess even if drenched in sweat, rain and humiliation. After much consideration I went with an eyeliner that I'd used at my sister's eighties-themed hen party. Bright, almost violent green, it was MAC's Liquid Last in Aqualine, and it takes about three days to remove. It didn't budge an inch on the hen night, despite us spending hours learning a dance routine and making a pop video to Whitney Houston's 'I Wanna Dance with Somebody'. I was still finding neon sparkles on my pillow for days afterwards, so I had absolute faith that this eyeliner would last a marathon. My faith was not misplaced. Despite at least an hour's downpour I am still wearing it in all of the grinning finish-line photographs taken on the day. Sure, it looks a little demented, but I was proud to have clung to a little disco glitter despite the horrors of the day.

Eyelashes

False eyelashes for running can feel very 'Jane Fonda workout video', a mere step away from streaks of brickish bronzer high on cheekbones and full lip gloss. But if your lashes are

301

as translucent as mine you can look like an albino rabbit in finishing photos and mascara applied six hours earlier simply isn't going to make the distance. I'm not suggesting you apply falsies the morning of the race, which would be altogether too stressful, but I have become somewhat devoted to an occasional twirl with semi-permanent eyelashes, done professionally in a salon. Applied individually to your own lashes they make you wake up looking like Brigitte Bardot and are almost impossible to remove until they 'grow off' with your own lashes. They are a firm marathon friend and I save the requisite cash to make sure that I can have a set on for big events.

Moisturiser

Running does extraordinary things to one's skin. As someone who has always had very dry skin I had anticipated a few extra hours a week spent outside would leave it more parchment-like than ever. In fact the opposite happens. The boost of circulating blood as well as the sweat pumping out of my pores gives me a glow that no product has been able to replicate. The salt of a good sweat is an incomparable exfoliant, as is the sea spray that regularly blasts my face on seafront runs.

But dry skin can be grim on long runs and during the winter I can feel rather battered. Clinique's Moisture Surge is my solution.

SPF

As I've already touched upon earlier, despite the scare-mongering about running making you look older, there is only one aspect to running that can age you: the sun. Hours spent under its glare in summer or winter can be terribly detrimental to the skin. I find it a little difficult to care too much about my skin ageing given that, well, I am ageing. But nor am I brimming with enthusiasm for a leathery face. That and a cap to keep the rays off your face.

A cap

The ultimate runner's beauty accessory, it hides you from the sun and it removes the dilemma about what to do with your hair.

Hair grips

A conundrum I have yet to solve fully. A ponytail can swish about against the momentum you're trying to run with, a fringe can flap and fall in your eyes, short hair can become wild and unpredictable. Over the years I have relied on a selection of caps, clips and Alice bands to keep wisps of hair from making me murderous when I should be enjoying running with the wind behind me. Elasticated cloth hairbands just ping straight off the back of my head and get lost in a bush. Buns unravel, no matter how many pins you put in them. Having tried everything I can think of I conclude that the best thing for keeping stray hairs under wraps are old-fashioned plaits. I run almost Mormon-style. Yes, it's something of a girl-woman look once you're over twenty-five, but then if your motives are entirely practical, as mine are, I reckon it's OK.

Packing for the Big Event

By the time the weekend of my first London Marathon came by I was in a state of such high anxiety that I am amazed anyone was still interested enough in my mission to turn up and support me. Perhaps my most neurotic behaviour was manifesting itself in my preparations for the morning of the Big Day. I had become so terrified of forgetting something that for two whole weeks before I had an immaculate display of everything I needed to take laid out over half of my sitting-room floor. The trouble was I kept having to use some of the things I'd need (my wallet, my trainers, my house keys) so I had developed a complicated Post-it note system where different colours stood in for what I was using. Looking back I have often thought that I had gone entirely mad, but in hindsight it was not a completely irrational fear. After all I was about to leave my home and try to cross one of the world's largest capital cities with *none of my stuff*. Not even a little knapsack like Dick Whittington, or a knackered Jaguar like in *Withnail and I*. As I've already described, you can feel very vulnerable handing over your bag before the race. It's gone, on a big truck, for hours. Your house keys, your ID, the lot. What I didn't know that first time is that the system they employ to get it back to you — particularly at the London Marathon — is awe-inspiring. On the day you register you are given a large, heavy-duty plastic bag with a huge number pinned to it. And on marathon day you have that same number pinned on you, so the chaps on the van can see you coming at the end, find your bag while you're being given your medal and goodie bag and then present it to you as if by magic. 'My bag!' I gasped that first time. 'How did you . . . ?'

For what must have been the 2343rd time that day he pointed at the two corresponding numbers, patted my arm and said, 'Well done, you must be very tired.' I was, but I was also happy to have my bag back.

Here's what you'll want to find in yours:

Warm, comfortable clothes

When you finish a long run your body starts to do some quite weird things, the likes of which I have only ever experienced during some of my most epic hangovers. You will be covered in sweat, probably looking as if you have just emerged from a shower even if you haven't made use of the cooling roadside showers en route. When you stop running it's very common to start shivering, even if it isn't cold or raining. I enjoy selecting my most luxuriously baggy clothes to put on when I'm reunited with my bag. A nice wide-necked sweatshirt and some tracksuit bottoms with a stretchy rollover waistband are the dream. Peel off any layers you think dignity will permit (I'm always happy to stand around in a sports bra at this point, they're way bigger than bikini tops) then shove the baggies on over the remainder of your running kit as soon as you can.

A pair of oversized socks/flip-flops

The degree to which feet swell over the course of a marathon is truly extraordinary, and trying to put any kind of shoe on once you've removed your trainers is like trying to stuff a baby back up the birth canal once it's crying in your arms. Huge socks that can be gently eased over throbbing feet are the order of the day here, even if you have to walk on a bit of pavement in them. If it's going to be hot, take flip-flops instead.

Compression socks, worn to ease the ache caused by blood gathering in the lower legs after long runs, are significantly harder to get on, and can be stretched delicately over your throbbing calves and feet once you have got home and showered.

Food that isn't too sweet

After months of training, carb monitoring and water slurping you might feel that a huge bag of Haribo will be exactly what you'll want to treat yourself with at the end of your marathon. Think again. The toxic combination of sweating, breathing through your mouth and eating and drinking sticky glucose products for hours on end over the course of the marathon will mean your teeth will feel coated with sugar and your stomach will probably be rumbling in revolt already. At most races they tend to give you even more sweets as they hand you your medal and T-shirt, so it is more likely to be oatcakes, nuts or crisps that you will crave. Crisps aren't ideal for the whole 'thousands of bags shoved on lorries and lugged across town' bit though.

Water isn't too important as there is generally a lot of it about at the finish line of big events, but you might want to have a bottle in there just in case.

Loo roll/wipes

There are just going to be so many places beyond the obvious that you'll want to wipe: your forehead, your feet, your sticky sticky hands, under your arms, behind your ears. Basically you will feel like a child who has just encountered his first Calippo and you will want to freshen up as much as possible until you reach a shower.

Painkillers/anti-inflammatories

Even if you have no injuries and aren't expecting any, taking some ibuprofen immediately after finishing a race can help your aching muscles and battered joints recover. Remember, medical staff at events will not give these to runners, as I learned to my cost. And it's always worth having some to share with others.

Tampax

If you are a first-time marathoner there is quite a strong chance that training will have confused your menstrual cycle a little. Anything could happen. Even if it doesn't, tampons make useful cotton-woolly tools to mop up all sorts of other cuts and grazes that might be incurred en route.

Phone

If you're not running with it you don't want to leave it behind. The London Marathon in particular can create a sort of 'New Year's Eve 1999 everyone on earth is texting at the same moment' log jam, but even so it is worth being in with a shot of contacting loved ones to either find them at the end or let them know you have made it.

Wallet

Even if you think you're not going to need any, because you've thought of everything you could possibly need, it's always worth taking some cash or a card, so you can either catch the cab home you thought you would do without, buy the pint you were sure you wouldn't feel like, or simply gain access to the petrol station bathroom that you hoped you wouldn't need on the way home.

Travel card/car keys
As above. No one should put more effort into getting to a start line than getting home from the finishing line.

Keys
Don't lock yourself out. It would be the world's biggest known case of 'FML' to be metres away from your bath and bed, yet unable to get into them.

Here's what you should have left the house with and discarded once used:

Baggy, disposable clothes
There can be up to an hour of standing around at large events between you needing to check your bag in and actually crossing the starting line. At the London Marathon in particular, with its huge numbers and non-competitive

310

fancy dress runners, it can take well over half an hour for slower runners to actually get within sight of the Start sign. If it's cold or raining you're going to want to be keeping warm for this dawdling. It is beyond grim to start a race shivering, with muscles as tightly wound as your nerves. The best thing to do is either scrounge your brother's/boyfriend's/father's skankiest painting clothes or go to a charity shop and spend £2–3 on a pair of baggy tracksuit bottoms and a hoodie that you don't mind throwing off, never to be seen again, once you're well under way and warm enough. It seems profligate, but most people do it and the races are well prepared for it. Before the starting pistol has even been fired there are charity representatives picking the items up by the side of the road and whisking them off to a better home. It's a rather lovely system, unless no one's let you know about it.

Bin liners
Second-hand hoodies will keep you warm, but they won't keep you dry. Bin liners will. Yes, it sounds a little early Vivienne Westwood dressing the Slits, but it's an incomparably practical system. Just peel one off from your roll under the sink, cut a gap in the bottom that's big enough to fit your head through,

fold it up and pop it in your bag. If there's a downpour while you're waiting you can put it over your head. The bag will come down to about your knees and keep your kit dry. As you approach the starting line you can slip it off and chuck it to the side. I tend to take a couple in case I see someone without getting drenched. It would make a great, if nerdy 'meet-cute'. This has yet to happen.

Banana/oatcakes/water

You might not want or need any of these things, but it's always worth having them, if only to share. By the time you reach the starting pens breakfast can seem like a long time ago, especially if you've had a long journey. Lunch will seem even further away. Nutritionally I am not sure I have ever needed the snacks I've eaten just before setting off, but I have always eaten them, in the spirit of not dying of the sudden and terrifying malnutrition I am usually resigned to encountering by this stage on the way.

Vaseline

I tend to put a big scoop into an old make-up container that has been through the dish-washer. It's good to have to hand in case any straps or seams need relubricating, or just to put on dry lips if it's a windy day. Again it is considerate to take a bit extra in case someone else is in need, and I pop it in a bin before setting off.

A biro

I have forgotten to fill in the Next of Kin details on my running number more than once, and now like to keep a crappy old biro in my sports bag just in case. Make sure it's not anything inky which might run if it rains. Again it's easy to bin before setting off as it's been especially selected for its 'nearly at the end of life'-ness anyway.

Your running number

In the five years I have been running the design of everything from water bottles to hair grips has improved almost beyond compare. Yet running numbers remain infuriatingly unchanged. How has no one tackled this? I despise them. They serve an invaluable purpose: they are your ID from the moment you surrender your bag until you retrieve it, or in case of a security emergency, and they carry contact and medical details in case of injury. Yet, given the slickness of almost everything else involved in public racing, they seem almost obnoxiously cumbersome. I often catch my wrists on the flapping fabric when I'm pumping my arms back and forth as I tackle a hill, and I have ruined a couple of tops by sweating through the fabric only to have the ink bleed off the back of the number. It is also impossible to affix the number if you have boobs. Men are fine, they just pin it onto their nice smooth man chests, popping it right above the stripe of their running club or sponsor vest. But women, women are different. They have to affix it over their stomach area where things are flatter. This is also an area that you can't see if you have boobs, as well as an area you don't really want to be blindly jabbing at with safety pins when you're already juddering with nerves. I've had to resort to asking women I've never met to help me out and am now resigned to pinning it to my top the night before, by lying on my back in my chosen running top like an anxious, carby ladybird, marking the spots where the pins need to go with a finger dipped in some water, taking the top off and then pinning the number on while the wet dots are still visible.

If men had boobs there would be another way. Oh yes.

Safety pins

For the mind-blowingly old-school method of affixing the aforementioned number to your running top. I hope with all my heart that one day they'll no longer be needed on lists like this. I keep a small bag of them in my sports bag at all times.

Glucose

These seem utterly disgusting and completely contradictory to all received ideas on health or weight loss. But running nine-minute miles for four hours uses over 3000 calories and you're going to need to replace them, fast. In the 1980s my father used to eat chalky Lucozade pellets for extra energy. It was the greatest of treats to be allowed to have a corner of one. Unadulterated glucose, it sent us into an immediate frenzy of hyperactivity, second only to Kendal Mint Cake. By the time I ran my first marathon they were replaced by glucose gels — sachets of pure glucose in a disgusting gloopy consistency. You have to rip the top off the sachet and suck the grim contents out as you run. Invariably your tense fist will squeeze too tight, leaving you with a spurt of overspill that brings an enthusiastic teenage boy to mind and leaves your hand sticky for the rest of the run. These days I prefer to get my glucose in the form of jelly beans. Lucozade make them, and even traditional brands like Jelly Belly make sporty versions of their standard jelly beans. These are significantly simpler to ration than the jizzy gels, and are easier to carry around as well. At some races they give them out, but not all, and they provide an invaluable boost when all else seems lost.

Painkillers

It is received medical wisdom that you shouldn't run with an injury, or take painkillers in order to mask it. I absolutely agree with this advice. But I have learned the hard way that sometimes you can hurt yourself on the way round, or see someone else in pain, and having a couple of ibuprofen tucked into a little pocket can make you feel invincible even if you don't end up using them. Again it is easy to feel as if you have entirely lost your grip on reality while doing this, but it's worth cutting the exact number that you need out of the blister pack and cutting round them to leave nice smooth curving edges. A pointy corner that doesn't seem like a big deal on your bedroom counter can seem like a tiny satanic dagger once it's been jabbing into your hip through your pocket for three hours. The rest of the packet can go in the bag that will meet you at the finish line.

Phone/sports watch

Not everyone likes to run with their phone, preferring to be reunited with it post-race. But I tend to use mine to monitor how my pace and distance are coming along, particularly as the mathematics involved seem to get exponentially more complicated the further I run. It's the flick of a thumb to check texts and tweets from there. I didn't realise how valuable it was until I ran the Brighton Half Marathon last year and one of the mile markers was in the wrong place. While I was trembling with rage as I saw my stats saying I'd run half a marathon while I was still a few hundred metres from the finish line, revenge was sweet the next day when a huge proportion of runners complained en masse and the marathon organisers ended up amending everyone's times. This proved to me that whether it's with a sports watch or an app, even if you are a mathematical genius it's always worth recording your own stats in a public event, rather than relying on timing chips alone. And if you don't want the distractions of a phone most people run with a watch and/or heart rate monitor.

18

The Magical Secret

'We run, not because we think it is doing us good, but because we enjoy it and cannot help ourselves . . . The more restricted our society and work become, the more necessary it will be to find some outlet for this craving for freedom. No one can say, 'You must not run faster than this, or jump higher than that.' The human spirit is indomitable.'
Sir Roger Bannister

That chapter title was a bit of a lie. Increasingly I am approached by people who want to start running but haven't, as if there is a magic secret they're waiting to be told. There really isn't. As every runner I admire has told me, from Paula Radcliffe to my dad, the only secret is that there is none. You just have to start running. But, in summary, here are the ten things I wish I had known when I started. As you'll see, much of it was advice from my father which took a little while to sink in.

1) Lacing up your trainers and leaving the house is the hardest moment of any run. You never regret it once you are en route. (Length of time ignored: one year.)

2) Nothing is ever as bad as your first time. No other run will induce that level of fear and pain. There are legions of people who believe that every run will feel like that first time. It never does.

3) Cover your feet in Vaseline each time you run for longer than about fifteen minutes. Not only will it stop blisters, especially if it rains, but it will mean deliciously moisturised feet on your return. (Length of time ignored: two years.)

4) Running in the rain is not perilous, but actually quite good fun. It totally proves the adage about there being no such thing as the wrong weather, just the wrong clothing.

5) Don't eat too much before a run. Two bananas and a three-egg omelette are not necessary. It's just more to carry

around with you. You are a healthy woman, not an elite athlete, so you have plenty of reserves. (Length of time ignored: three years.)

6) There is an extraordinary market in D+ cup sports bras which has clearly employed the skills of some of the world's finest engineers. And if you rub Vaseline around your ribcage you'll be even more comfortable.

7) Don't pay any attention to anyone else once you're out there: they are either absorbed by what they are doing or looking in admiration. If you can't do that, get a cap. (Length of time ignored: two-and-a-half years.)

8) No one cares what you look like when you're running. Ever. Whether it's clean, cool or baggy. Those first few runs *do* feel as if you're thundering down a catwalk surrounded by sneering professionals, but after a while that feeling disappears as you realise you just want to be comfortable — and that the rare glance might not be so bad after all.

9) Stop stealing my running socks, they don't fit you properly! (Length of time ignored: five years and counting.)

10) You might enjoy it.

Acknowledgements

This book would never have existed if I had never crossed a finish line, so first and most heartfelt thanks must go to those who have been at my side as I did it, particularly my beloved Lottie Lambert, the magnificent Julia Raeside, Nick Brady and Lila Frei. And of course Sarah Ballard, my immaculate 'fragent', without whom I would have dared to neither run nor write, and with whom I am proud to cross the publication finish line.

The first steps of any book induce exhaustion, exhilaration, wobbly legs and a terrifying sense that one's bowels could go at any time. So beginning a book *about* those feelings was particularly tricky. Early supporters were invaluable, with their unwavering belief that the book itself and the exploits it entailed were both possible and worthwhile. Thank you, Damian Barr, Clare Bennett, Grace Dent, Sophie Heawood, Jojo Moyes, Melissa Marshall, Caitlin Moran, David Nicholls, Rachel Roberts, Jessica Ruston, Polly Samson, Craig Taylor and of course my ever-patient mother and her Olympic-level cheering skills.

Once the project was up and running I

only reached its many finish lines with the incomparable support of a rum collection of characters who were as consistent with their merciless teasing as they were with their steadfast pre-race cooking, mid-race cheering and post-race consoling skills. Thank you, Courtney Arumugam, Carol Biss, Joanna Ellis, Janey, Urmee Khan, Oli Lambert, Vanessa Langford, Jon Macqueen, Mike Moran, Joel Morris, Sarah Morgan, Kerry & Kieron Moyles, Geri O'Donohoe, Matthew Park, Jack Ruston, Julian Stockton, Jon Taylor, Eva Wiseman and darling Louis, who provided such inspiration.

I am indebted to several people for their practical advice, and for taking me seriously no matter how many childlike turns of phrase, ridiculous procrastination techniques or ludicrous questions I employed. They are all masters of their professions and have been friends to me when I needed it. Thank you, Anna Barnsley, Kurt Hoyte at Run in Hove, Debs Hughes, Adam Kann, Josie Mitchell, Jay Stephenson-Clarke, Jo Taylor, Tim Weeks, and everyone at beautiful Café Coho in Brighton, where I both started and finished the book.

And thank you to everyone at Hutchinson and United Agents, particularly Jocasta Hamilton, Zoe Ross and Lara Hughes Young, who have been consistent in their support of the book, my writing and my determination not to have a pink book jacket. It has meant an enormous amount.

We do hope that you have enjoyed reading this large print book.

Did you know that all of our titles are available for purchase?

We publish a wide range of high quality large print books including:
Romances, Mysteries, Classics
General Fiction
Non Fiction and Westerns

Special interest titles available in large print are:
The Little Oxford Dictionary
Music Book
Song Book
Hymn Book
Service Book

Also available from us courtesy of Oxford University Press:
Young Readers' Dictionary
(large print edition)
Young Readers' Thesaurus
(large print edition)

For further information or a free brochure, please contact us at:
Ulverscroft Large Print Books Ltd.,
The Green, Bradgate Road, Anstey,
Leicester, LE7 7FU, England.
Tel: (00 44) 0116 236 4325
Fax: (00 44) 0116 234 0205

Other titles published by Ulverscroft:

SMOKE GETS IN YOUR EYES

Caitlin Doughty

Most people go to great lengths to avoid thinking about death, but when Caitlin Doughty — a young woman with a degree in medieval history and a flair for the macabre — took a job at Westwind Cremation & Burial, her morbid curiosity turned into her life's work. Leading us behind the black curtain of her profession, Caitlin takes us into a world of vivid characters (both living and deceased) and bizarre details (exactly how a flaming skull looks) — and explores the funeral practices of historic and contemporary cultures, calling for better ways of dealing with death and our dead.

SHOP GIRL

Mary Portas

Young Mary Newton, born into a large Irish family in a small Watford semi, is always getting into trouble. When she isn't choking back fits of giggles at Holy Communion or eating Chappie dog food for a bet, she's accidentally setting fire to the local school. Whilst money is scarce, these are good times, and everything revolves around the force of nature that is Theresa, Mary's mum. But when tragedy unexpectedly blows this world apart, a new chapter in Mary's life opens up. She takes to the camp and glamour of Harrods window dressing like a duck to water — and Mary, Queen of Shops is born . . .

TSUNAMI KIDS

Paul Forkan and Rob Forkan

Siblings Rob, Paul, Mattie and Rosie were orphaned in the 2004 Boxing Day tsunami. They subsequently made a harrowing 200km trek across the devastated country of Sri Lanka, trying to discover the fate of their parents. The bravery and ingenuity they displayed was a direct result of their unique upbringing. Taken out of school at a young age, they had received an unconventional global education, learning independence and emotional resilience . . . Almost a decade after the disaster, the eldest brothers, Rob and Paul, created the multinational brand Gandys, and established the charitable foundation Orphans for Orphans. This is the story of their journey from survival to success.